Tentmakers

Tentmakers

Multivocational Ministry in Western Society

Editors

James W. Watson

Narry F. Santos

Foreword by Jeff Christopherson

WIPF & STOCK · Eugene, Oregon

TENTMAKERS

Multivocational Ministry in Western Society

Copyright © 2022 Wipf and Stock Publishers. All rights reserved. Except for brief quotations in critical publications or reviews, no part of this book may be reproduced in any manner without prior written permission from the publisher. Write: Permissions, Wipf and Stock Publishers, 199 W. 8th Ave., Suite 3, Eugene, OR 97401.

Wipf & Stock
An Imprint of Wipf and Stock Publishers
199 W. 8th Ave., Suite 3
Eugene, OR 97401

www.wipfandstock.com

PAPERBACK ISBN: 978-1-6667-3997-8
HARDCOVER ISBN: 978-1-6667-3998-5
EBOOK ISBN: 978-1-6667-3999-2

SEPTEMBER 23, 2022 3:45 PM

Unless otherwise indicated, all Scripture references are from the New Revised Standard Version Bible, copyright © 1989 National Council of the Churches of Christ in the United States of America. Used by permission. All rights reserved worldwide.

Scripture references marked NIV are taken from taken from New International Version, ESV®, NIV® Copyright ©1973, 1978, 1984, 2011 by Biblica, Inc.® Used by permission. All rights reserved worldwide.

Contents

List of Tables and Figures | vii

List of Contributors | ix

Foreword | xi
    JEFF CHRISTOPHERSON

Preface | xv
    NARRY F. SANTOS

Introduction: Canadian Tentmakers and the Future of Ministry in Western Societies | xiv
    JAMES W. WATSON

PART 1: CANADIAN MULTIVOCATIONAL MINISTRY PROJECT

1. Patterns among Canadian Multivocational Ministers | 3
    JAMES W. WATSON

2. Multivocational by Choice: What Difference Does It Make? | 16
    WANDA MALCOLM, BETH ANNE FISHER, AND ELVIRA PRUSACZYK

PART 2: BIBLICAL AND THEOLOGICAL REFLECTIONS ON TENTMAKING

3. What Multivocational Ministers Can Learn from Paul's Tentmaking Experience | 45
    NARRY F. SANTOS

4. Charism, Vocation, and Work: Theological Reflections on Tentmaking | 59
    JAMES E. PEDLAR

Part 3: Issues Arising from Multivocational Ministry

5 The Tentmaking Home as Sanctuary | 71
   MARILYN DRAPER AND MARK D. CHAPMAN

6 Sabbath Rest in Multivocational Ministry | 82
   MARK D. CHAPMAN

7 Tending to the Tentmakers | 94
   JARED SIEBERT

Part 4: Personal Reflections from Multivocational Ministers

8 Multi-Role Ministry as a Salvation Army Officer | 107
   MICHAEL W. PUDDICOMBE

9 Being a Professor in the City and a Pastor in the Country | 117
   JAMES TYLER ROBERTSON

10 Twenty-Eight Years and Counting | 126
   CAM ROXBURGH

11 Ministry or Career? An Unnecessary Dichotomy | 133
   AMY BRATTON AND ASHOOR YOUSIF

List of Tables and Figures

List of Tables

Table 1: Regular Role Commitments of Multivocational Ministers

Table 2: PAI Factors and Sample Items

Table 3: NAI Factors and Sample Items

Table 4: Descriptive HSS Results

Table 5: HSS Profile Comparison

Table 6: CMMP HSS Profiles

Table 7: CMMP Top Five Core Satisfiers

Table 8: CMMP Top Five Core Stressors

List of Figures

Figure 1: Frequency/Intensity Quadrant Model

Figure 2: Mean HSS Subscale Scores for Choose-to-Leave versus Choose-to-Stay CMMP Participants

Figure 3: Mean Core-Satisfier Percentage Scores for Choose-to-Leave versus Choose-to-Stay CMMP Participants

Figure 4: Mean Satisfaction Scores, Stress Scores, and Satisfaction–Stress Ratio Scores for Choose-to-Leave versus Choose-to-Stay CMMP Participants

Contributors

Amy Bratton, MCS, ThM. New Leaf Network operations manager, contributing editor of the New Leaf Writers Collective, and adjunct faculty at Rocky Mountain College.

Mark D. Chapman, BRS, BA, MA, PhD. Director of DMin program and associate professor of research methods at Tyndale University.

Marilyn Draper, BJ, MDiv, PhD. Assistant professor of practical theology at Tyndale University.

Beth Anne Fisher, BA, MDiv, PhD candidate. Research project manager for the Wellness Project @ Wycliffe.

Wanda Malcolm, BA, MA, PhD. Professor of pastoral psychology at Wycliffe College.

James E. Pedlar, BA (Hons), MDiv, PhD. Donald N. and Kathleen G. Bastian Chair of Wesley Studies and associate professor of theology at Tyndale University.

Michael W. Puddicombe, BA, MA, PhD candidate. Officer in The Salvation Army Canada and Bermuda.

Elvira Prusaczyk, BA, MA, PhD candidate. Wellness Project @ Wycliffe statistical consultant.

James Tyler Robertson, BRS, MDiv, PhD. Online development and design at Tyndale University and pastor of Mountsberg and Westover Baptist Churches.

Cam Roxburgh, BA, MDiv, DMin. National director of Forge Canada and senior pastor of Southside Community Church.

Contributors

Narry F. Santos, BS, MDiv, STM, PhD. Assistant professor of Christian ministry and intercultural leadership and senior pastor of Greenhills Christian Fellowship Peel and York.

Jared Siebert, BTh. Director of New Leaf Network and national director for church development for the Free Methodist Church in Canada.

James W. Watson, BA, MDiv, PhD. Corps health and planting consultant for The Salvation Army Canada and Bermuda and instructor at Tyndale University.

Ashoor Yousif, BEng, MTS, MA, PhD. Assistant professor of Christian history at Tyndale University and pastor of Middle East Baptist Church.

Foreword

Jeff Christopherson

COULD THERE BE A MORE important topic for the church in the West to grapple with, both theologically and missiologically, than the subject of this book? I think not. Is there currently a better researched and more biblically based approach to accessing this subject? Not that I am aware of. Drs. James Watson and Narry Santos have assembled a treasure trove of biblical scholarship, qualitative research, and practical applications; I found myself constantly "amening" my way through their work. And so, before I get too far into this foreword, let me offer this warning: read this book at your own risk. *It will be difficult for anyone to maintain a status quo mindset*, one that is committed to the primacy of a professional clergy, after an open-hearted and open-minded reading of their analysis.

As editors on this subject, missiologists Watson and Santos are uniquely qualified. Watson—researcher, missiologist, and tenured catalytic voice in Canada—exposes with clarity the current realities of the mission field and the mission force. He has spent his lifetime across a varied denominational spectrum helping to solve the Canadian missional dilemma. Santos has the academic credentials and the practical experience that qualifies his expertise. His global perspective of movements laid alongside his apostolic efforts in helping the church in the West to reimagine a more biblical and hopeful future sets the tone for their work. Together, Watson and Santos have assembled an experienced cadre of voices that prescribe a path forward derived from both thoughtful research and personal experience.

Why is this important?

As the founding leader of the Send Network, I helped to focus a very large, conservative denomination on the task of evangelistic church planting amid the realities of secularity. We focused our energies on cities, the places that had the least gospel access. We concentrated our work on thirty-two cities across North America that comprised 80 percent of its population. Thirty-two urban areas that had the lowest church-to-population ratios in North America. Thirty-two areas that had the least Christian memory and were often considered to be the most missiologically difficult.

Next, we began to prepare the missionary workforce. Having spent my lifetime in this space, I began to call on friends, colleagues, and longtime heroes to help us build a system that could prepare a diverse mission force for the post-Christian realities that would be facing them. Our assessments, training, ongoing coaching, and planter care became the gold standard for church planting in North America. We were excited about the days ahead.

Were we successful? Well, it depends on how you measure things.

We planted about seven hundred churches each year, with most of them being found in places where church planters of our tribe rarely went in the past. So, that was a big win. Previously, I could go to a large city like Toronto or Boston and gather all our church planters together in a coffee shop. Today, when I visit those cities, we need to rent a hotel ballroom for such a gathering. And did they last? Yes. On average, we had well over an 80 percent survival rate after five years—something that our denomination had never experienced.

So, quantitatively, yes, we were successful.

But digging a bit deeper, I began to notice something more troubling.

If I asked the question "Did our planters feel successful?" the answer would look quite different. I discovered that over 50 percent of our planters, after their five years of funding were completed, were, in fact, "multivocational" pastors. Over half of our planters required outside employment or support to balance the books. And this wasn't how they had seen their preferred future as they had set out into their church-planting dream. But it was their current reality. And many felt like church-planting failures because of it.

Understanding the difficulties in church planting, part of our screening, training, coaching, and care centered around the value of tenacity. And these were very tenacious leaders—resolute missionaries who endured hardship as tough gospel soldiers and carved out gospel communities from some of the most inhospitable environments. Yet, did they feel successful? No, they didn't. Why? Because they couldn't produce the financial success story that they had envisioned.

By 2016, we felt we had to give language and support to the phenomenon we were observing. The only word we had in our ecclesiastical lexicon

Foreword

was "bivocationalism," and with it came the constant reinforcement of failure. The prefix "bi-" is most often used to connote division or separation: bisection, bifurcation, and being bifocal. Bivocational pastors often see themselves with two competing preoccupations and would readily shed the "less spiritual" one if the "spiritual" one paid better.

We decided to invent a term that would help us define our preferred future. The prefix "co-," coming from the Latin *com*, means "together." If planters could see themselves as covocational leaders called to Jesus' mission as experienced in both the "sacred" and the "secular" settings, would they still feel like failures?

But the problem was bigger than I imagined.

In 2017, Ed Stetzer and I founded the Send Institute, an interdenominational church-planting and evangelism think tank operating out of Wheaton College that represented seventy-two denominations and networks. To my surprise, except for a tiny minority of denominations that concentrated large resources and planted a relatively small number of new churches, most groups were seeing the same kind of results. And often, to a much greater degree. It seems that as religious memory has evaporated throughout most geographies, the comparatively recent historical concept of a professional clergy has become much more difficult to attain. And the problem is universally experienced.

So, perhaps it is time to rethink our ecclesiological prejudices and adopt a more first-century approach to our twenty-first-century conundrum. Whether it's our personal preference or not, multivocationalism is the current reality for an increasing number of pastors and church planters in the West. And the pace of adoption is only mounting. For some, it is unavoidable, but for others, it is a missiological choice—a choice, when fully embraced, reveals patterns and rhythms that sync much better with the New Testament pattern than our more modern iterations.

So, I encourage you to read *Tentmakers: Multivocational Ministry in Western Society*. See how the Holy Spirit reorders, shifts, and challenges you.

Because our future is here.

Jeff Christopherson
cofounder and missiologist,
Send Institute;
executive director,
Church Planting Canada
(and multivocational pastor, The Sanctuary)

Preface

NARRY F. SANTOS

THE GENESIS OF THIS edited volume was sparked in 2018 when James W. Watson and I were part of a ministry project that allowed us to share common passions of study and research. One common passion that surfaced in this conversation and other ensuing discussions was about tentmaking in Canada. Anecdotally, we sensed that this is a growing North American reality in church and ministry, especially in church planting. In our own circles of ministry, we kept hearing of the need to engage in bivocational approaches in pastoral leadership. But we knew there was a dire need to do research on the current tentmaking realities across Canada.

Watson's rich experience in qualitative and community-based research was pivotal in spearheading this research project and gathering a robust multidisciplinary research team for the Canadian Multivocational Ministry Project (CMMP). The research team brought a broad range of perspectives and expertise in research methodology and practice. The following disciplines provided such variety from different professors and graduate students: missiology and intercultural studies (Santos and Watson), New Testament (Santos), practical theology (Marilyn Draper, Beth Ann Fisher, Michael Puddicombe, Jared Siebert), psychology (Wanda Malcolm), and religious studies (Mark Chapman). These research team members were invited to speak into the interview design, conduct interviews, serve as analysts, or give comments on the analysis of written reports. Moreover, the executive team of Watson (cochair) and Siebert (cochair), Cam Roxburgh, and Santos discussed the trajectory of the research and opportunities for engaging the Canadian church.

While the research team conducted the majority of the interviews, we would like to thank Tracey-Ann Van Brenk for her willingness to serve

Preface

as interviewer. Amy Bratton and Alanna Johnson of New Leaf Network directed the administration and management of the research data, including the time-consuming transcription of interviews (with the added help of Melissa Summach and Watson). We also received the added blessing of forging a partnership with the Wellness Project @ Wycliffe, which uses online questionnaires to assess wellness in congregational ministry. Malcolm served as the lead researcher for the Wellness Project, while Watson served as lead researcher for the CMMP.

Th whole research project became a reality through the support and encouragement of a wide range of Canadian Christian leaders. We are grateful for the participation of these leaders. Specifically, we appreciate the executive and research team members of Forge Canada, The Free Methodist Church in Canada, Lausanne Movement Canada, The Salvation Army Canada and Bermuda, Tyndale Intercultural Ministry Center, Tyndale University, and the Wellness Project @ Wycliffe. New Leaf Network deserves special recognition for being the administrative partner in managing the transcription of interviews, data storage, and promotion of resources. We also thank the following partners who financially supported this project: The Free Methodist Church in Canada, Mennonite Church Canada, The Salvation Army Canada and Bermuda, and Vision Ministries Canada.[1]

Having seen the completion of the research report and the analysis of the wellness and interview findings, Watson and I (along with the executive team) desired to extend the mileage of such significant study on multivocational ministry in Canada. This edited volume is the result of that desire. We wanted scholars (in New Testament, theology, practical theology, religious studies, and psychology), researchers, and reflective practitioners of multivocational ministry to engage the findings of the research project. The chapter contributors graciously accepted our invitation to reflect on tentmaking in relation to their field of study, church context, or multivocational ministry experience. To them we express our heartfelt thanks. Additionally, we extend our gratitude to Chris Spinks (Wipf & Stock editor) for believing in this book project.

Finally, we give thanks for the Holy Spirit's guidance throughout the research project and writing of this volume, for Jesus's inspiration, and the Father's calling of many pastoral leaders and church planters who have stepped out in faith toward a fulfilling, challenging, and strategic multivocational ministry.

1. To get a full copy of the CMMP research report, kindly visit this link: https://www.canadianmultivocationalministry.ca.

Introduction

Canadian Tentmakers and the Future of Ministry in Western Societies

James W. Watson

Tentmaking has a long tradition in the Christian church. The terminology is associated with Paul, Aquila, and Priscilla, as they plied a trade of making tents and shared the gospel and catalyzed the initiation of churches.[1] Serving as a congregational leader and also engaging in another occupation has been noted throughout the history of the church in the writing or practice of Christian thinkers such as Tertullian (second to third centuries), Basil of Cappadocia and Chrysostom (fourth century), Columba (sixth century), Augustine of Canterbury (seventh century), Martin Luther (sixteenth century), Matteo Ricci (seventeenth century), Count Nicholas von Zinzendorf and John Wesley (eighteenth century), and Roland Allen (nineteenth to twentieth centuries).[2] From a contemporary perspective, consideration of tentmaking in Western societies is drawing an increasing amount of attention, in part due to concerns about decreasing church attendance and starting new, sustainable churches.[3]

---

1. Watson and Santos, "Tentmaking," 140–42.

2. Gustafson, "Church History of Bivo," paras. 11–12; Lee, "Historical Perspective," 101–19; Samushonga, "Theological Reflection," 66–80.

3. Watson and Santos, "Tentmaking," 131–39.

Introduction

Multiple shifts in Western societies are generating creative ways to initiate and maintain churches. Secularization addresses many areas of life, but for the purpose of this text, it will be considered as societal trends negatively affecting personal belief as well as participation in religious organizations.[4] Considerable attention has been given to congregational declines in Australia, Canada, Western Europe, New Zealand, and the United States of America (USA).[5] Global migration has impacted congregations in Western societies as they have developed to serve immigrant communities.[6] The history and outcomes of transnational migration are complex and vary substantially from country to country (with differences in immigration policies, migration flows, and settlement processes).[7] While it is not possible to review all that has been discussed about secularization and global migration, it is important to note that these trends have been identified as having significant implications for Western societies, providing some background for understanding what the church is facing.

Canada provides an excellent context for considering the experience of tentmakers because of these contextual factors. Ongoing decline in church attendance and the rising demographic category of "religious nones," who indicate no religious affiliation, place Canada among many Western societies that are directly affected by these trends.[8] Immigration is a key factor in Canada's population-growth strategy for economic stability, with projections that by 2036, people born outside of Canada may make up 24–30 percent of the country's population.[9] The largest Canadian city of Toronto compares to Brussels, Auckland, Sydney, Los Angeles, Singapore, London, New York, and Melborne, with each having at least a third of the population being foreign born.[10] A significant proportion of immigrants to Canada have been Christians (relative to the Canadian population), contributing to a trend running counter to secularization.[11] Migration is contributing

---

4. Thiessen, *Meaning of Sunday*, 3–30.

5. Bouma and Halafoff, "Australia's Changing Religious Profile"; Bullivant, "Europe's Young Adults," 5–11; Thiessen and Wilkins-Laflamme, *None of the Above*, 2–25.

6. Jackson and Passarelli, *Mapping Migration*, 40–127; Pepper et al., "Social Cohesion in Australia"; Wan and Casey, *Church Planting among Immigrants*, 16–20.

7. Hanciles, *Beyond Christendom*, 180–206.

8. Reimer and Hiemstra. "Gains/Losses"; Thiessen and Wilkins-Laflamme, *None of the Above*, 2–25.

9. Morency et al., *Immigration and Diversity*, 27–28.

10. Lee, *World Migration Report*, 39.

11. Connor, *Immigrant Faith*, 20; Reimer and Hiemstra, "Gains/Losses."

Introduction

to the need for new churches that reflect different cultural expressions of Christian faith. This study of multivocational ministry reflects on Canada's current conditions to explore elements of the tentmaking experience.

Some explorations of the contributions that multivocational leaders make to the churches in Western societies have been started. European churches have benefited from leaders who also hold other jobs for financial support.[12] There has been American interest in bivocational ministry from many different denominational circles, with surveys indicating that about a third of American churches have volunteer or part-time paid leadership, with variation in proportions among different traditions (and debate as to where there are recent increases).[13] We know that part-time work of Canadian congregational staff has been slightly on the rise, but there is much more to learn.[14] The interest in multivocational leadership is fueled by issues that are seemingly becoming more common—issues that have the potential to drive these trends in the future.

Long-established churches are wrestling with concerns about decline and looking for pragmatic (or outreach-oriented) ways to sustain ministry. New churches are being started by leaders concerned about how to engage meaningfully in local communities while managing the costs associated with start-up. Recent migrants—some of whom are arriving as Christians—are creating new churches while also facing the challenges of becoming settled in a new country (and supporting their congregants in their settlement process).[15] Each of these scenarios points to the potential of tentmakers making substantial contributions.[16]

Canada has provided an excellent environment for conversing with tentmakers. It has had leaders serving in multivocational pastoral roles for many years and in a variety of forms.[17] While there has been some recognition of the presence of part-time or bivocational leaders, there is currently a lack of information, and some tentmakers indicate that they feel their

---

12. Samushonga, "European Theological Pentecostal Perspective."
13. Chaves and Eagle, "Religious Congregations," 75; Carroll, *God's Potters*, 79–83. There may not be an overall increase in the USA, with the exception of certain segments of Christian denominations (see Perry et al., "Are Bivocational Clergy?").
14. Reimer and Hiemstra, "Part-Time Employment."
15. Reimer et al., "Christian Churches"; Samushonga, "Theological Reflection."
16. Watson and Santos, "Tentmaking."
17. Ambrose, "Living by Faith"; Gustafson, "Church History of Bivo," para. 19.

approach to ministry is perceived as an unusual or substandard arrangement.¹⁸ There is an interest among leaders and ministry instructors to have a more common understanding of this approach to ministry, as it provides one way forward for the Canadian church in the midst of an uncertain future.

The language of tentmaking has been chosen for this study because of the biblical references to Paul as a leatherworker or tentmaker.¹⁹ While there are some distinctions, the authors have had opportunity to use "bivocational" or "multivocational ministry" as generally synonymous with "tentmaking." "Multivocational" is a term that was selected after the Canadian fieldwork was completed because a number of the interviewees were committed to more than two significant forms of work. There are a number of other terms that may have specific meaning for a denominational tradition but largely describe a similar concept—a congregational minister or missionary who also has other paid employment.²⁰

The terms "bivocational," "covocational," "multivocational," and "tentmaking" often have overlapping definitions but are sometimes used in specific ways. "Bivocational" and "multivocational" tend to be used in a general sense, implying that there is other employment beyond congregational leadership, but the relationship to calling as a minister of the gospel is ambiguous. "Covocational" and "tentmaking" are frequently cited in missiological literature and may have very specific connotations. "Covocational" implies a shared direction and mission between the different forms of work.²¹ Tentmaking is a topic of biblical study because of its use in the New Testament narrative but is sometimes linked to business-as-mission approaches in global contexts (where Christian witness may be complicated because of laws or customs regarding religion).²² There are other terms, often grounded in the particular polity or vocabulary of a Christian tradition.²³ "Multivocational" is the primary term used for the research project in order to explore the different ways individual ministers have organized their work (many of whom have more than two commitments). "Tentmaker"

18. Watson et al., *Canadian Multivocational*, 19.
19. Hock, "Paul's Social Class"; Watson and Santos, "Tentmaking"; Lai, *Tentmaking*, 11–13; Kruger, *Tentmaking*, 143–49.
20. Samushonga, "Theological Reflection."
21. Brisco, *Covocational*.
22. Hock, "Paul's Social Class"; Lai, *Tentmaking*, 1–6.
23. Samushonga, "European Theological Pentecostal Perspective," 3–4.

Introduction

is the designation chosen for this volume because of its connection to the early church, as we examine the application of this form of ministry to the future of Western society.

Regardless of the terms used, there are some general issues raised by writers on this topic. Some are very pragmatic, while others combine practical and theological dimensions. The available literature which is specific to this form of ministry is both diverse in its application and limited in depth in terms of general social-science investigation. Much of the literature is focused on biblical reflection and/or personal anecdotes contributing to strategic propositions.[24] Within Canada, there has been some student or denominational research that is helpful for pointing to the need for understanding and raising issues.[25] A review of literature from other Western countries shows a broader range of research; however, such research is still limited.[26] These (primarily qualitative-research) projects have highlighted issues of calling, work/life balance, concerns about lack of comradery or general understanding, and increased ministry relevance with local contextual awareness (via employment outside of the congregation).

Research

The core of this book is mixed-methods research with a community-based research approach: the Canadian Multivocational Ministry Project (CMMP). The research combines qualitative (focus group and semi-structured interviews) and quantitative (online questionnaires and statistical analysis) methods. The Wellness Project @ Wycliffe (WP@W) provided the online questionnaire and additional data beyond the interviewees (see chapter 2), while a focus group in Calgary (Alberta, Canada) assisted in the formation of questions for the interviews. In community-based research parameters, the design and analysis engaged leaders who were, or are, tentmakers alongside the other researchers and administrators.[27] There is an intentional focus for the research to contribute constructively to tentmaker

---

24. Some helpful examples are Bickers, *Art and Practice*; Brisco, *Covocational Church Planting*; Eddington, *Bivocational*.

25. Some helpful examples are Jones, *Who Am I?*; Lambkin, *Bi-vocational Skunkworks*.

26. Bentley, "Perspectives"; *Bivocational Ministry*; *Bivocational and Part-Time*; Peterson, *Working Priests*; Samushonga, "Theological Reflection"; Smith, *Effective Strategies*.

27. Ochocka and Janzen, "Breathing Life."

Introduction

ministry. The three primary research questions for the project demonstrate this approach:

1. What are key features of the diverse expressions of bivocational ministry in Canada? What are challenges? What are opportunities?
2. What are significant biblical and theological emphases to consider?
3. How can promotion of the opportunities and resourcing of the challenges take place strategically?

These three questions formed the basis of the research. Open-ended questions (developed for the semi-structured interviews) provided an opportunity for the interviewees to share details that the researchers may not have known to ask for, contributing to the breadth of findings (see chapter 2). Of the forty interviewees, thirty-two completed the WP@W online questionnaire. This allowed the questionnaire to address congregational leadership while the interviews facilitated discussion about the other work, recognition of theological frameworks, and recommendations of resources.[28] The WP@W analysis (in chapter 2) has expanded beyond these interviewees to contrast univocational and multivocational ministers who have completed the online questionnaire outside of the CMMP.

Progression of Chapters in the Book

The chapter contributors are a mix of researchers, writers, and tentmakers. The research has benefitted from former or current tentmakers who took part in design, data gathering, analysis, and reflection. While much of the bivocational literature available focuses on personal experience, a major contribution of this book is the combination of research and experience. The chapters progress from findings of the research (part 1), to general biblical and theological insights (part 2), to specific reflections on issues raised by the research (part 3), and to personal reflection on the experience of tentmaking (part 4). This progression both allows for general understanding and specific issues to be presented and gives the reader access directly to the reflections of current tentmakers. The objective is to provide the reader with the opportunity to benefit from the reflections of others and to reflect personally on the implications. The dream is that this book would

---

28. Malcolm et al., "Ministry-Specific Stress"; Malcolm et al., "Complexity of Assessing."

INTRODUCTION

contribute to further exploration, encourage further research or writing, and launch others into the multivocational adventure.

Part 1 introduces the Canadian research and its findings. Chapter 1 serves as my overview of the qualitative research. The focus in this chapter is placed on distinctive themes arising from the interviews with tentmakers. The reasons why tentmakers were performing multiple kinds of work often emerged from the descriptions of their work. The WP@W provides comparative analysis of multivocational and univocational leaders in chapter 2. The research of Malcolm, Fisher, and Prusaczyk advances in a similar fashion to an expedition, with examination of one facet of the similarities between these different ministry approaches leading to the next investigation. Their conclusions deserve further thought, particularly regarding the emotional cost of multivocational leadership.

Part 2 deals with selected biblical and theological insights on tentmaking. Chapter 3 places tentmaking in its New Testament context. As both a practitioner and a biblical scholar, Narry Santos provides grounding on the tentmaking experience of the apostle Paul and culls practical lessons for contemporary multivocational ministers. Chapter 4 offers a theological examination of charism, vocation, and work. James Pedlar's historical reflection creates a framework for understanding that all Christians are implicated in this ministry. The theological basis for fundamental ways of thinking about ministry and work opens up possibilities for envisioning what can be possible for the future.

Part 3 discusses three specific issues raised by the research: "home," Sabbath, and care for tentmakers. Chapter 5 presents an investigation of the concept of "home" for tentmakers. The home is identified in some of the interviews as a pinch point in their busy schedules, so Marilyn Draper and Mark Chapman point to theological themes for understanding homelife— themes that can help multivocational leaders avoid some difficulties. Draper's own experience provides illustrative examples of how theological insight and life in the home connect. Chapman unpacks some of the research and theological literature on Sabbath in chapter 6. As might be expected, the busy lives of tentmakers can result in challenges finding time for rest and restoration. Chapman outlines the issues facing multivocational leaders and draws from a depth of reflection on the ideals for Sabbath. "Tending to the Tentmakers" (chapter 7) takes insights from the research and provides guidance for supporting tentmaking colleagues. Jared Siebert outlines opportunities and challenges at the personal, local-church, and

Introduction

denominational levels. This provides a multilayered perspective on the future of mission in Canada.

Part 4 shares the personal reflections of contemporary tentmaking practitioners. Chapter 8 presents theological reflection by Major Michael Puddicombe regarding his experience in multi-role ministry. While The Salvation Army provides a very specific mission direction and way of operating, he prompts reflection on how we are shaped by our ecclesiological traditions and the opportunities they present. His role as a practical theologian provides a path for others to follow.

In chapter 9, James Robertson's personal reflection on working at a university in the city and ministering to a two-point charge (two small churches) in the countryside demonstrates how such a context allows for personal development. The research project gave numerous examples of how pastors could reflect on their experiences in their workplaces as having a profound impact on themselves as well as their ministry. This chapter provides an opportunity to understand how someone integrates these diverse experiences. In chapter 10, Cam Roxburgh outlines personal learning from almost three decades of tentmaking. The pitfalls encountered in multivocational ministry are laid out in detail with the hope that we all can learn from this experience. Since his objective is not to dissuade people from taking the multivicational path, Roxburgh closes his chapter by pointing out the benefits of tentmaking. This balanced perspective builds vision for the future. Finally, in chapter 11, Amy Bratton weaves together an interview with Ashoor Yousif and research insights to unpack how the life experience of a pastor and engineer/professor points to major issues to be considered for multivocational churches. Yousif's journey with tentmaking allows for understanding of some of the intentional choices that churches can make to embrace a holistic understanding of work and mission.

The future of ministry in Western societies such as Canada is not predetermined by our traditions or preconceived notions of congregational life. Biblical and theological reflection on the basic principles of charism and vocation as well as contemporary wisdom from practitioners opens up the issues we can address. The objective of tentmaking is not only sustainability but richness in engagement. The lives of our multivocational colleagues and the opportunities for transformation in their communities drive the need for prayerful imagination and practical creativity. As the Holy Spirit inspires us to live out our calling, we will be surprised by the possibilities.

Introduction

Bibliography

Ambrose, Linda M. "Living by Faith: Family Life and Ministry in the Diary of a Pentecostal Woman Preacher, 1940–1960." *Historical Papers: Canadian Society of Church History*, 2015, 93–112. https://historicalpapers.journals.yorku.ca/index.php/historicalpapers/article/view/39665/35970.

Bentley, Kristen Plinke. "Perspectives of Bi-Vocational Ministry: Emerging Themes in Bi-Vocational Ministry Research at Lexington Theological Seminary." *Lexington Theological Quarterly* 48 (2018) 115–51. https://lextheo.edu/wp-content/uploads/2021/09/j-4-Perspectives-of-Bi-Vocational-Ministry.pdf.

Bickers, Dennis W. *The Art and Practice of Bivocational Ministry: A Pastor's Guide*. Kansas City, MO: Beacon Hill, 2013.

Bivocational Ministry. Richmond: Earlham School of Religion, 2016. https://esr.earlham.edu/research/ecffm/bivocational (resource discontinued).

Bouma, Gary D., and Anna Halafoff. "Australia's Changing Religious Profile—Rising Nones and Pentecostals, Declining British Protestants in Superdiversity: Views from the 2016 Census." *Journal for the Academic Study of Religion* 30 (2017) 129–43. https://doi.org/10.1558/jasr.34826.

Brisco, Brad. *Covocational Church Planting: Aligning Your Marketplace Calling and the Mission of God*. Alpharetta, GA: Send Network, 2018.

Bullivant, Stephen. "Europe's Young Adults and Religion: Findings from the European Social Survey (2014–16) to Inform the 2018 Synod of Bishops." London: Benedict XVI Centre for Religion and Society, 2018. https://research.stmarys.ac.uk/id/eprint/2280.

Carroll, Jackson W. *God's Potters: Pastoral Leadership and the Shaping of Congregations*. Grand Rapids: Eerdmans, 2006.

Chaves, Mark, and Alison Eagle. "Religious Congregations in 21st Century America." *National Congregations Study* (2015) 55–106. https://sites.duke.edu/ncsweb/files/2019/02/NCSIII_report_final.pdf.

Christian Reformed Church in North America. "Study of Bivocationality Task Force." 2020. https://www.faithaliveresources.org/Products/830135/study-of-bivocationality-task-force.aspx.

Connor, Phillip. *Immigrant Faith: Patterns of Immigrant Religion in the United States, Canada, and Western Europe*. New York: New York University Press, 2014.

Donaldson, Marc B. "A Means to an End: The Sustainability of Bivocational Ministry." DMin diss., Asbury Theological Seminary, 2016. https://place.asburyseminary.edu/ecommonsatsdissertations/829/.

Eddington, Mark D. W. *Bivocational: Returning to the Roots of Ministry*. New York: Church Publishing, 2018. https://www.bivocational.church/2018/01/04/introduction/.

Gustafson, David M. "A Church History of Bivo: Tentmaking from the Beginning until Now." *EFCA Today*, Spring 2016. https://www.efcatoday.org/story/church-history-bivo.

Hanciles, Jehu J. *Beyond Christendom: Globalization, African Migration and the Transformation of the West*. Maryknoll, NY: Orbis, 2008.

Hartwell, Jay, and the Issue Group at the 2004 Forum for World Evangelization. "Lausanne Occasional Paper 39: The Local Church in Mission." Presented at the 2004 Forum for World Evangelization, hosted by the Lausanne Committee for World Evangelization

Introduction

in Pattaya, Thailand, between September 29 and October 5, 2004. https://lausanne.org/content/lop/local-church-mission-lop-39.

Hock, Ronald F. "The Problem of Paul's Social Class: Further Reflections." In *Paul's World*, edited by Stanley E. Porter, 7–18. Pauline Studies 4. Leiden, Netherlands: Brill, 2008.

Jackson, Darrell, and Alessia Passarelli. *Mapping Migration, Mapping Churches' Responses in Europe*. Geneva, Switzerland: World Council of Churches, 2016.

Jones, Kate. "Who Am I? Bi-vocational Ministers and Pastoral Identity." MDiv diss., Atlantic School of Theology, 2017. https://library2.smu.ca/handle/01/27050.

Kruger, Kurt T. *Tentmaking: A Misunderstood Missiological Method*. Eugene, OR: Wipf & Stock, 2020.

Lai, Patrick. *Tentmaking: The Life and Work of Business as Missions*. Downers Grove, IL: InterVarsity, 2005.

Lambkin, Andy. *Bi-vocational Skunkworks: An Initial Exploration of Bi-vocational Ministry within the C&MA in Canada*. National Implementers Network, n.d.

Lee, June J. H., et al., eds. *World Migration Report 2015: Migrants and Cities; New Partnerships to Manage Mobility*. Geneva, Switzerland: International Organization for Migration, 2015. https://publications.iom.int/system/files/pdf/wmr2015_en.pdf.

Lee, Samuel. "Historical Perspective on Entrepreneurial Church Planting." In *Entrepreneurial Church Planting*, edited by W. Jay Moon and Fredrick J. Long, 101–20. Wilmore, KY: GlossaHouse, 2018.

Malcolm, Wanda M., et al. "The Complexity of Assessing Ministry-Specific Satisfaction and Stress." *Journal of Psychology and Theology* (2021) 1–20. https://doi.org/10.1177/00916471211021921.

Malcolm, Wanda M., et al. "Measuring Ministry-Specific Stress and Satisfaction: The Psychometric Properties of the Positive and Negative Aspects Inventories." *Journal of Psychology and Theology* 47 (2019) 313–27. https://doi.org/10.1177/0091647119837018.

Mennonite Church USA. *Bivocational and Part-Time Pastor Survey Results*. 2006. https://mennoniteusa.org/wp-content/uploads/2015/03/SurveyofMennonitePastors.pdf.

Morency, Jean-Dominique, et al. *Immigration and Diversity: Population Projections for Canada and Its Regions, 2011 to 2036*. Ottawa: Statistics Canada, 2017.

Ochocka, Joanna, and Rich Janzen. "Breathing Life into Theory: Illustrations of Community-Based Research—Hallmarks, Functions and Phases." *Gateways: International Journal of Community Research and Engagement* 7 (2014) 18–33. https://doi.org/10.5130/ijcre.v7i1.3486.

Pepper, Miriam, et al. "Social Cohesion in Australia: Comparing Church and Community." *Religions* 10 (2019) 605–27. https://www.mdpi.com/2077-1444/10/11/605.

Perry, Samuel L., and Cyrus Schleifer. "Are Bivocational Clergy Becoming the New Normal? An Analysis of Current Population Survey Data, 1996–2017." *Journal for the Scientific Study of Religion* 58 (2019) 513–25. https://doi.org/10.1111/jssr.12593.

Peterson, Aaron. "Working Priests: Improving the Care for Vineyard Bivocational Pastors." DMin diss., George Fox University, 2018. https://digitalcommons.georgefox.edu/dmin/254/.

Reimer, Sam, and Rick Hiemstra. "The Gains/Losses of Canadian Religious Groups from Immigration: Immigration Flows, Attendance and Switching." *Studies in Religion/Sciences Religieuses* 47 (2018) 327–44. https://doi.org/10.1177/0008429818754786.

———. "The Rise of Part-Time Employment in Canadian Christian Churches." *Studies in Religion* 44 (2015) 356–77. https://doi.org/10.1177/0008429815595811.

Introduction

Reimer, Sam, et al. "Christian Churches and Immigrant Support in Canada: An Organizational Ecology Perspective." *Review of Religious Research* 58 (2016) 495–513. https://doi.org/10.1007/s13644-016-0252-7.

Samushonga, Hartness M. "A European Theological Pentecostal Perspective to Bivocational Ministry." *Journal of the European Pentecostal Theological Association* 40 (2020) 144–59. https://doi.org/10.1080/18124461.2020.1795421.

———. "A Theological Reflection of Bivocational Pastoral Ministry: A Personal Reflective Account of a Decade of Bivocational Ministry Practice Experience." *Practical Theology* 12 (2019) 66–80. https://doi.org/10.1080/1756073X.2019.1575040.

Smith, Gregory Harris. "Effective Strategies for Bi-vocational Ministry." DMin diss., Talbot School of Theology, 2014. https://media.proquest.com/media/hms/ORIG/2/qZv7H?_s=ot2m7dpTb6sQLu7OdtZQYhTben4%3D.

Thiessen, Joel. *The Meaning of Sunday: The Practice of Belief in a Secular Age.* Montreal: McGill-Queen's University Press, 2015.

Thiessen, Joel, and Sarah Wilkins-Laflamme. *None of the Above: Nonreligious Identity in the US and Canada.* New York: New York University Press, 2020.

Wan, Enoch, and Anthony Casey. *Church Planting among Immigrants in US Urban Centers: The "Where," "Why," and "How" of Diaspora Missiology in Action.* Portland, OR: Institute of Diaspora Studies–USA Western Seminary, 2014.

Watson, James W., and Narry F. Santos. "Tentmaking: Creative Mission Opportunities within a Secularizing Canadian Society." In *Mission and Evangelism in a Secularizing World*, edited by Narry Santos and Mark Naylor, 131–48. Eugene, OR: Pickwick, 2019.

Watson, James W., et al. *Canadian Multivocational Ministry Project: Research Report.* 2020. https://www.canadianmultivocationalministry.ca/report.

Part 1

Canadian Multivocational Ministry Project

1

Patterns among Canadian Multivocational Ministers

James W. Watson

There is conversation developing among pastoral, seminary, and denominational leaders addressing both the potential for multivocational leadership and a lack of understanding regarding the different experiences of tentmaking. The Canadian Multivocational Ministry Project research was organized around a community-based research approach both to ground understanding in experience and point to ways in which insight might provide direction in the future.[1] With the limited research literature available (see the introduction for a review), the intent of the research was to be exploratory—to open issues for consideration and imagine possible responses for the future.

Research Methods

Interviews with the forty participants were recorded in video calls and transcribed. Interviewees who have had many different forms of additional work beyond their congregational responsibilities were intentionally sought out. The sampling of individuals to take part in the interviews was both convenient and strategic. While partners in the project provided access to some pastoral leaders, others were invited through a web page for

1. Ochocka and Janzen, "Breathing Life."

the research, and the sampling was strategic in that there were goals for diversity of other employment, representation across the regions of Canada, and gender difference, and attention was given to the birth country of interviewees for a multicultural country such as Canada (with thirty interviews being suggested as a minimum for cross-cultural research).[2]

Who Were Interviewed?

The interviewees were men (twenty-four) and women (sixteen) from across Canada with representation from British Columbia, Alberta, Saskatchewan, Manitoba, Ontario, Quebec, the Maritimes, and Newfoundland. While about one-fifth of the participants were born outside of Canada, similar to the national demographics, this does not fully represent the cultural complexity of the participants.[3] There were tentmakers who identified their congregations as multicultural—some congregations were primarily serving first-generation and second-generation immigrants; one leader who was ministering in French, which was the leader's third language; and one preacher who ministered in an Asian language, though the preacher's first language was English. The majority of congregations represented were urban, approximating the population distribution in Canada. There was a mix of different denominations, with the largest proportions coming from the three primary funders of the research: The Free Methodist Church in Canada, Mennonite Church Canada, and The Salvation Army Canada and Bermuda. Additional traditions represented were from Baptist, Christian and Missionary Alliance, Pentecostal, and independent backgrounds. The leaders indicated a variety of different kinds of congregations—some as small as house churches, or "incarnational communities," and some large enough to have multiple staff.

The pastoral roles were varied; some were in the process of starting new churches (church planters), while others were in established congregations. While many identified that they were paid part-time by the congregation, some were lead or sole ministers; others were co-pastors; and some were on a ministry team as associate pastors or serving in specialized roles (e.g., youth pastor). There were also volunteer congregational leaders—one, who belonged to a congregation that had a Sunday-worship-gathering style

---

2. Hagaman and Wutich, "How Many Interviews."
3. "Immigration and Ethnocultural Diversity."

(much larger than a house church), indicated that they had operated with no paid staff for about half a century.

As the selection process focused on finding diverse combinations of work, there was a wide range of roles portrayed by the interviewees. Table 1 shows the substantial, regular role commitments that were identified.

Table 1. Regular Role Commitments of Multivocational Ministers

Administrator (social services, health care)	Manager (housing/rental)
Author/writer	Manager (landscaping)
Business analyst (government)	Manager (social-awareness program)
Carpenter (furniture)	Manager (retail)
Chaplain (health care)	Marketer (freelance)
Chaplain (military)	Music coordinator (choir/worship)
Chaplain (natural resources/industry)	Musician
Chaplain (police)	Network coordinator (social issues)
Coach (church planting)	Occupational therapist
Company owner (entrepreneur)	Outreach worker (social services)
Consultant (airlines)	Painter (residential/industrial)
Consultant (information technology)	Personal support worker
Consultant (health care)	Public relations (fundraising, communication)
Denominational staff	School bus driver
Executive director (social services)	Shelter worker (social services)
Editor	Spiritual director
Educational assistant	Teacher (elementary level)
Farmer	Technician (lab equipment)
Foster parent (group home)	Truck driver
Funeral officiant	Volunteer (community radio)
Housing coordinator (ministry)	Volunteer (community theatre)
Luthier	Wedding officiant

It appears that very few of the tentmakers' positions were minimum wage, and a number of the roles (but not all) required specific training, credentials, experience, or apprenticeship. Note that not all of these roles represent a one-to-one relationship with church leadership; some individuals had more than one additional commitment. Also, not every possible combination is represented in this list. As a personal example, I went directly from seminary to volunteer with a church plant and, in the process, worked as an administrator half-time for an established church and half-time for an agribusiness start-up. Later chapters provide personal reflection from pastors who have worked in parachurch and university settings.

Themes

The interviewees were very generous with their comments, explanations, and theological reflection.[4] While specific questions were asked about weekly schedules and the positives or negatives of multivocational ministry, many other issues were raised by the participants, and some can be inferred from their descriptions. During analysis, the question has been raised as to what is distinct about multivocational ministry compared to univocational ministry.[5] This is a challenging issue to address based on the interviews (qualitative research), because the focus was on revealing issues that affect multivocational ministers, not on comparing issues with univocational leaders (see chapter 2 for comparative analysis). Essentially, both have the same, general "vocation" (a life commitment to following Christ) and have a similar range of ministry tasks; the challenge is to identify unique elements of multivocational life. While there are a broad range of themes from the research, this chapter will focus on those that enhance this distinctive perspective.

Time

When we asked tentmakers how they organized their time during a typical week, we learned several things about their complicated schedules. In general, the leaders interviewed had full schedules ranging from forty to seventy hours invested weekly in their combined employment and significant volunteer commitments (with limited outliers above seventy hours). This raises concerns about making time for family and rest (see chapters 5 and 6). Some schedules were built around predictable and regular

---

4. For additional findings, please see Watson et al., *Canadian Multicultural Ministry Project*.

5. Special thanks to Mark Chapman and Joel Thiessen for discussion of this issue on several occasions and in several formats.

commitments, while other leaders stated that they valued flexibility (which implied a certain amount of control on their part), and some were seasonal (e.g., farming and education). Regarding differences between multivocational and univocational ministers, this is one of the most obvious differences; there are additional scheduling complications that tentmakers must consider.

There were very few common patterns among the weekly schedules; time commitments were clearly specific to the individual. One of the leaders interviewed was working night shifts at homeless shelters and doing weekend work as personal support worker. The night shift enabled afternoons with the youth outreach to connect with high school students when they were available. One of the co-pastors worked a full-time government office job, complete with commute (pre-pandemic), but made use of evenings for prayer, mentoring, and youth group. In both cases, reliable predictability was a factor, either the regularity of the time required to connect with youth on their own terms or the office hours around which the ministry flowed. One co-pastor worked three chaplaincy positions: regional health-care center (hospital) on Mondays, telehealth on Tuesdays, and home visits for palliative care on Fridays. A few business owners were in the study—they described the balance of being master of the work schedule and the additional responsibilities that they uniquely bore for their companies. One church planter emphasized that both the plant itself and the freelance marketing contracts provided flexibility. While there were general rhythms of work and gathering, the specifics would change from week to week.

Unique Fit

"Unique fit" is a concept developed from analysis of the research data regarding how the tentmakers described their combination of roles. While each pastoral position may be considered unique because of the individual facets of a minister's talents and experiences with the congregation's social and spiritual context, multivocational ministry adds the layer of work outside of the congregation. What emerged from the way the multivocational leaders described the rationales or motivations for their particular combinations of work revealed patterns of meaningfulness.

One of the issues to be resolved is the motivation or perception of value that a tentmaker relates to the additional work. "Conflicted" is the term used to describe situations described by the tentmakers when they are seriously considering leaving one of their positions. The value of having multiple roles has decreased. The combined work is considered to be unnecessary or unsustainable. If the leader determines that the effort required to maintain a second career is not worth the benefits, then they can become monovocational. One situation where a pastor identified complications was that a school bus route was taken on to provide additional income for higher education. Once the degree was completed, then both the decreased need for additional work and the increased desire for a full-time pastoral position meant that there would likely be a change in employment in the future. Some situations were more complicated. One church planter was working as a delivery driver as well as a chaplain in a local industry. The plan was to exit the driving career as the new congregation developed; however, the once-a-month chaplaincy commitment was considered by the planter to be nonnegotiable. It was an industry that was part of the family history of the planter, and the ministry opportunities available through serving the workers in this way were deemed too important.

One basic assumption often encountered during conversations about tentmaking is that the additional work is done "for the money." This is generally true, as there must be enough financial benefit to justify the time spent committed to the task. This was identified by interviewees who mentioned specifically the benefit to the congregation or family of the additional financial support. A limited number indicated that the amount of money provided was substantial, which gave them freedom to limit their hours or their dependence on financial support from the congregation. "Lucrative" is the term chosen to describe situations where the trade-off between time and money seems reasonable. This implies that the money serves a specific purpose and the schedules are compatible. One company owner who served on a leadership team for a missional congregation seemed to structure the relationships between the different commitments in a compartmentalized fashion—the business commitments were distinct and separate from the investment of time in a congregation in a neighborhood strongly impacted by poverty. A pastor serving a small church where the language of worship was not English (or French) also provided worship coordination for an English church; the schedules were compatible because the worship services were at different times on the weekend.

Two alternative patterns that emerged are *complementary* and *integrated* understandings of the purpose of additional employment. The other work may provide a complementary benefit for the pastor personally, or it may be integrated with the mission of the congregation. The example of the planter who wanted to honor family tradition is one example of a complementary relationship with secondary employment. Another pastor was apprenticed in the family workshop in order to nurture current relationships. One interviewee shared that ministry and planes had been long-term passions, and reaching a point in his airline career where forming a consulting business allowed time to serve a congregation as the sole part-time pastor was an answer to prayer. A pastoral leader who also served on the denominational-organization regional-staff team found that experience in the local congregation informed decisions made at the regional office, and contact with other congregations inspired creative thinking in the local context. A youth pastor in a major urban center and a church planter in a medium-sized city both worked in public education, and both identified relationships with coworkers as being a grounding experience for them. A pastor of a rural congregation who was also a farmer made it known that there were opportunities for cross-pollination between the two roles—pastoral reflection happened on the tractor seat, and the pastoral role was never lost in the interaction with neighbors and customers.

While all interviewees were asked how congregational leadership and their other job worked together, a few explained how additional work was integrated with the mission emphases of their church. Integration of relational witness was a priority both practically and theologically. In general, the participants in the study who emphasized the role of congregational mission in their other work also indicated the importance of intentional integration. Some were responsible for holistic mission centers that required connections between church life and responsibilities for social services and fundraising. These leaders, when they described their work week, were very busy (as were others working close to full-time hours in addition to congregational leadership). The work they were doing provided a variety of contacts—both with people facing crises or having particular needs (emergency-food access, supplemental community meals, referrals to specialized services to assist with housing, addictions, advocacy for health or social supports) and with people who were service providers or community leaders (for partnerships, funding access, or promotion of services). One leader, who acknowledged valuing having opportunities to engage in spiritual conversation with people connected to social-service supports offered through the ministry center, also raised concerns over the time commitments in administering professional social services.

PART 1 | CANADIAN MULTIVOCATIONAL MINISTRY PROJECT

    One church planter, who was also a landscaping-company manager, claimed that there were opportunities to be seized in the day-to-day of working life. Who would anticipate that landscaping would be missional? This raises the question: Are certain forms of work conducive to integration with congregational mission, or does the intentionality of the leader create the opportunities for sharing of faith, regardless of the form of employment? While certain types of work can create many relational contacts (social-service outreach, local sales or service, networking as a consultant, frontline hospitality positions) and some can enable long-term relationships (managers, team leaders, supervisors), the missional intent of the leader may be essential for either developing deeper relationships with those contacts or creating opportunities in situations where mission connections may not be obvious. Attention to the *missio Dei* directs us to extend God's blessing to everyone with holistic care for the whole person, but relational connections and spiritual conversations are foundational to offering the way of Jesus.[6] This is demonstrated in the Gospels by Jesus' interaction with a wide variety of people. Jesus instructs his followers to continue to make connections, discern opportunities for faith to be explored, and extend the blessing of God.

    A church planter who claimed that their family had been operating in this manner for a couple of decades (in more than one country) stated that they understood they were all on mission and that intentional integration was central. While operating an information-technology consulting firm with a handful of employees, the planter created opportunities for engaging in spiritual conversations with the employees of the client companies served by the firm. As the company is located in a highly secularized Canadian city, the working relationships allowed for an opportunity to get to know one another to determine when to enter into conversation about faith. This allowed the coworker to know the planter as an authentic and caring person and allowed the planter to discern if revealing their identity as "pastor" would be detrimental to their working relationship. As the pandemic has demonstrated, there is no way to accurately predict the future. God is sovereign and holds the future; however, if this degree of secularization becomes increasingly common, will this degree of intentionality be required?

---

    6. Genesis 12:3 provides a focal point for this global vision of blessing in the Old Testament.

Calling

Though important for all discussions of ministry, "calling" was a prominent feature of both the online-questionnaire responses and some of the very emphatic responses during the interviews. In the interviews, there was no distinct question about calling, but some of the respondents raised it as a prominent issue when addressing why they do what they do. In a few interviews, this was presented during discussion of challenges: their calling was an anchor in stormy seasons. The following words affirm the role of calling in the interviewees' ministry:

> Well, one of the first things I would want to say is that bivocational ministry is something that will only work if you have a very clear sense of call to the demands that you'll face. Because there is, you know, seasons and moments where bivocational/trivocational work, you're exhausted, you're depleted and it's that sense of calling that you rely on, the trust that God by Spirit is going to enable you and empower you, and that this is your reasonable act of service and love for God and for Jesus.

For some, it was a clarifying lens for examining what they were doing and affirming their specific direction. While it may be reassuringly simplistic to hope for a "one-size-fits-all" approach to tentmaking, the realities of tentmakers' lives point to the need for individual discernment in their reflection on calling. For those who laid claim to an "all-of-life" ministry mandate, they were, in effect, applying their calling as ministers of the gospel to the various different activities which made up their week (see chapter 4 for theological reflection on this topic).

Mission as All of Life

The discussion of whether or not it is theologically appropriate to believe in a sacred/secular divide was raised by some of the tentmakers in the study: "And when you work with a team of bivocational people who tend to be drawn that way anyway, you begin to not divide the sacred and secular quite so quickly." This was connected to their storytelling about sharing faith with people who were not part of the congregation. While there was some sensitivity expressed about identifying themselves as Christians or speaking about faith with others in the workplace, there were stories of how they would engage people spiritually. Some mentioned conversations about why they were pastors as well as having their other work; others explained that their work made them available to their coworkers as spiritual guides or allowed them to demonstrate God's love in deeply personal ways.

Some of the participants in the study explained how they encouraged all of their congregants to engage their Christian spirituality through the whole week. Their experience in other fields of work was advantageous for their teaching ministry to both reflect on the experiences of their coworkers' perspectives on life as well as to share with their congregation how their faith impacted their work week. Their multivocational lives allowed them to model how their faith impacted their understanding of their work.

Ecclesiology in Practice

How the congregation engages with faith, ministry, and work was addressed by a number of the interviewees in different ways. While no questions were specifically asked about their theology of the church (ecclesiology) or specific practices in congregational life, some descriptions were shared. While ecclesiology is commonly thought of as theological writing about the church, theological emphases can be discerned from the activities and patterns of organization as well.[7] This connectivity between theological ideals and typical practice deserves attention in conversations about effective ministry.

There were a few variations on the ecclesiological theme of the priesthood of all believers. This was described in different ways and obviously finds expression in different ways for different church traditions, but it is connected with the ideal that all of the congregation is to be engaged in ministry/mission. While some used the Old Testament language of a "kingdom of priests" and others referred to New Testament texts such as Ephesians (chapter 4) for exploration of roles, a number of the leaders explained how this was expressed in their congregations.

One of the pragmatic ways the emphasis on shared ministry was described in congregational life was the understanding of teamwork in leadership of the church. Many of the participants referred to their "team." One individual mentioned specifically that the local leadership board listened to them describe their various commitments on a regular basis and offered advice or revised ministry expectations to ensure a healthy ministry. Some suggested that having other work made the justification for shared leadership easier; everyone knew that the pastor had another job and could

---

7. Ammerman et al., *Studying Congregations*; Cameron et al., *Studying Local Churches*.

not be expected to do everything. A few mentioned that they had set up teams with specific responsibilities for congregational life (preaching, for example). A couple of the leaders offered their theology of stewardship as the basis for creating this ecclesial environment. Again, part of this was theological and part very practical; those who are part-time leaders only have so much time available to commit to congregational work. Erika Mills offered an eloquent summary in her interview.

> Where I land is my work is an expression of my createdness, my giftedness, how God has wired me to be. And so, my work is going to be most effective, most fulfilling, when I'm able to focus on those areas that I'm gifted at, and so I feel like it's an absolute luxury to be able to look at my week ... based on what is lifegiving, what is fruitful, and what is good stewardship of who God's created me ... when it's a part time job, people in the church need to understand that we can't do everything, that others in the congregation need to pick up some of the work and take responsibility, and so we're able to prioritize those areas that we're gifted in that we want to spend our energy on.[8]

Ideally, all churches would have ministry teams operating out of their giftedness with respect for the individual strengths of the pastor(s), but multivocational churches make a strong case for the necessity of this ecclesiological practice.

Looking to the Future

From what has been learned, what can be applied? The complexity of tentmakers' schedules means their unique configurations deserve attention. This is necessary as the tentmaker negotiates schedules with those for whom they are responsible (family, church, clients/employers/employees). For people who care about and support tentmakers, assisting them with their discernment of their unique fit and offering practical help to fill roles that complement their God-given charisms could make a difference. The tentmaking discussion needs to move beyond financial sustainability to meaningfulness, which ultimately may be the best foundation for sustainability.

---

8. According to community-based research principles, interviewees were given the option to have their names associated with their quotes if they so desired (rather than anonymity).

Considering the bigger picture, what does this mean for the church in Western societies? Global trends of globalization, secularization, and urbanization are creating environments that contribute to opportunities for tentmakers to learn internationally.[9] With the history of international mission and current migration patterns providing cross-fertilization of experiences, there is great potential for mutual learning. Local leaders can offer perspective on local job markets and the needs of society based on their multivocational experience, while immigrant Christian leaders can bring fresh eyes to the cultural and spiritual dynamics (as well as any prior tentmaking experience). While skill sets and strategies for schedules will vary widely, conversation about the theological themes of mission infusing all of life and the stewardship of the gifts of the congregation can be shared to inspire specific approaches. Embracing mission as a personal lifestyle and collaboration as the church community will advance the capacity of multivocational congregations.

While there will be challenges in the future, the diversity of combinations of work points to the variety of possibilities that the Holy Spirit can inspire. The wisdom of tentmakers deserves attention. Any possibility for providing platforms or forums for sharing of perspectives could be beneficial both to the tentmakers and to anyone who may be considering this direction for ministry. Our contributions to the future of the church will hinge on attention to the Lord's prompting and courage to consider these creative possibilities.

Questions for Reflection

1. What do you consider to be the most interesting research findings?
2. How would you discern "unique fit" for multivocational ministry?
3. How do the theological ideals of the priesthood of all believers and the stewardship of gifts apply in your context?

---

9. Hartwell and the Issue Group at the 2004 Forum for World Evangelization, "Local Church in Mission."

Bibliography

Ammerman, Nancy T., et al. *Studying Congregations: A New Handbook*. Nashville: Abingdon, 1998.

Cameron, Helen, et al. *Studying Local Churches: A Handbook*. London: SCM, 2005.

"Immigration and Ethnocultural Diversity: Key Results from the 2016 Census." October 25, 2017. https://www150.statcan.gc.ca/n1/daily-quotidien/171025/dq171025b-eng.htm.

Hagaman, Ashley K., and Amber Wutich. "How Many Interviews Are Enough to Identify Metathemes in Multisited and Cross-Cultural Research? Another Perspective on Guest, Bunce, and Johnson's (2006) Landmark Study." *Field Methods* 29 (2017) 23–41. https://doi.org/10.1177/1525822X16640447.

Hartwell, Jay, and the Issue Group at the 2004 Forum for World Evangelization. "Lausanne Occasional Paper 39: The Local Church in Mission." Presented at the 2004 Forum for World Evangelization, hosted by the Lausanne Committee for World Evangelization in Pattaya, Thailand, between September 29 and October 5, 2004. https://lausanne.org/content/lop/local-church-mission-lop-39.

Ochocka, Joanna, and Rich Janzen. "Breathing Life into Theory: Illustrations of Community-Based Research—Hallmarks, Functions and Phases." *Gateways: International Journal of Community Research and Engagement* 7 (2014) 18–33. https://doi.org/10.5130/ijcre.v7i1.3486.

Watson, James W., et al. *Canadian Multivocational Ministry Project: Research Report*. 2020. https://www.canadianmultivocationalministry.ca/report.

2

Multivocational by Choice
What Difference Does It Make?

WANDA MALCOLM, BETH ANNE FISHER,
AND ELVIRA PRUSACZYK

THE KEY PURPOSE OF this chapter is to take a closer look at the eroding and sustaining elements of multivocational ministry ("MV ministry" from here forward). The chapter builds on previous research involving over three hundred people engaged in ministry who contributed data in the form of responses to online questionnaires.[1] Our research rests on the assumption that effectively engaging in ministry work for years at a time requires intentional and consistent attention to all forms of wellness (physical, intellectual, psychological, spiritual, and vocational), especially when one understands their work to be sacred. Our goal is to gather knowledge that will support people in their efforts to cultivate and maintain vocational wellness.

In contrast to vocational wellness, professional burnout is "brought about by devotion to a cause, way of life, or relationship that [has] failed to produce the expected reward."[2] Christina Nerstad and her colleagues suggest that engagement itself can become a burnout risk factor when

---

1. Malcolm et al., "Measuring Ministry-Specific Stress"; Malcolm et al., "Complexity of Assessing."

2. Freudenberger and Richelson, *Burnout*, 13.

work-related demands exceed the resources needed to meet those demands.³ Julia Moeller and associates add that highly engaged people are more likely than unmotivated individuals to cope with increased demands by overextending both the energy and time they invest in their work.⁴ When this pattern is sustained over time, engagement becomes over-engagement and symptoms of burnout escalate. Although our research does not focus on assessing an individual's effectiveness, it is important to note that because ministry life calls for high levels of engagement and commitment, there is an elevated risk that both well-being and effectiveness will erode if persistent work demands exceed the personal and work-related resources available to meet those demands.⁵

In our exploration of vocational well-being, we have assumed that the absence of stress does not equate to satisfaction in one's work experience, nor does the absence of stress mean that a person is flourishing. We conceptualize stress and satisfaction as separate (though not unrelated) constructs and assume that there are ministry-life "satisfiers" that stand in contrast to the "stressors" that erode a person's capacity to enjoy a sustainable life of faithful ministry. The more opportunities there are to engage in the strongly positive elements of our work life, the more likely we are to thrive. By extension, the more often we are obligated to engage in the strongly negative elements of our work, the more likely we are to experience the downward spiral of stress, distress, and professional impairment.⁶

In addition to being mindful of the satisfiers and stressors of ministry life, it matters whether one perceives the demands of their work as a hindrance or challenge. The research team headed by Eean Crawford has shown that the risk of burnout increases when work demands are experienced as obstacles to achieving one's work-related goals (i.e., hindrances) and that markers of engagement increase when work demands are perceived as difficult but manageable requirements of the job (i.e., challenges).⁷

The research reported in this chapter involves an exploratory study comparing data provided by individuals engaged in MV ministry with data obtained from individuals whose work is carried out in a single setting

---

3. Nerstad et al., "Can Engagement Go Awry."
4. Moeller et al., "Highly Engaged."
5. Malcolm et al., "Measuring Ministry-Specific Stress"; Malcolm et al., "Complexity of Assessing."
6. Mikail, "Professional Self Care."
7. Crawford et al., "Linking Job Demands."

(univocational ministry, or "UV ministry" going forward). The focus is on the ways in which these individuals' experiences of ministry life may be contributing to vocational wellness or unwellness.

In the introduction to this book, James Watson provided a high-level overview of the state of the MV research literature. Because this is a new field of social-science research, most investigations have necessarily been either qualitative in nature or an empirical investigation of only a small set of factors. In the latter case, the relationship between those factors and burnout have most often been tested using the Maslach Burnout Inventory (MBI).[8] As is often true in a new field, it is graduate students who have led the way with their dissertation work. It is truly unfortunate that this has not translated into any publications in peer-reviewed social-science research journals. In fact, to our knowledge, Perry and Schleifer are the only researchers to have published the results of an empirical study that explicitly focuses on MV ministry.[9]

We are now taking the next step, researching indices of engagement (as described by Leiter and Maslach) as well as burnout and comparing data provided by MV ministry workers with data obtained from people engaged in UV ministry.[10] Equally important, we have compared both groups' MBI data with the norms published in the MBI manual to determine whether the data gathered is similar to or markedly different than data gathered from those involved in other human-services professions. Given the newness of this research field, the work described in this chapter is highly exploratory, and any initial conclusions drawn from it must be held tentatively as we await further confirmatory research.

Our ongoing interest in ministry-life wellness and stress made collaboration with the Canadian Multivocational Ministry Project ("CMMP" going forward) of great interest to us. Our previous research has shown that ministry life is a multifaceted experience in which no single aspect is universally present or essential to experiences of ministry-life satisfaction or stress.[11] Still, patterns of stress and satisfaction emerged, and we welcomed the opportunity to explore MV ministry experiences quantitatively as a complement to the qualitative work (described in chapter 1) of this

---

8. Maslach et al., *Maslach Burnout Inventory Manual*.
9. Perry and Schleifer, "Are Bivocational Clergy."
10. Leiter and Maslach, "Latent Burnout Profiles."
11. Malcolm et al., "Measuring Ministry-Specific Stress"; Malcolm et al., "Complexity of Assessing."

book. To that end, the individuals who agreed to participate in the CMMP qualitative research were also invited to participate in the Wellness Project @ Wycliffe, an ongoing program of empirical research designed to examine the ups and downs of ministry life. This allowed us to test the expectation that there would be overlaps and divergences in the experience of those engaged in MV ministry compared to those engaged in UV ministry.

Demographically, the 335 individuals involved in the Wellness Project @ Wycliffe to date were comprised of men (46 percent) and women (54 percent) who represented ordained (52 percent) and non-ordained (48 percent) ministry workers. Fifty-seven percent of the participants were between twenty and forty-nine years of age, and 43 percent were fifty years of age or older. Denominationally, the largest groups were Anglican (39 percent), Salvation Army (15 percent), Baptist (11 percent), and nondenominational (9 percent). The remaining 26 percent of the participants represent fourteen other denominations. When we began collaborating with the CMMP team, we added demographic questions that allowed us to identify the vocational status of the ministry workers. Of the 102 individuals who participated after we added the question about vocational status, 41 self-identified as being engaged in UV and 61 reported that they were involved in MV ministry. Of the 61 who said they were MV, 32 were CMMP participants and 29 were non-CMMP MV ministry workers.

The online questionnaires completed by participants in the Wellness Project @ Wycliffe included the Human Services Survey version of the MBI ("HSS" going forward) and two other questionnaires specifically developed for use in the Wellness Project @ Wycliffe—the Positive Aspects Inventory (PAI) and the Negative Aspects Inventory (NAI).[12]

Human Services Survey Version of the Maslach Burnout Inventory

The HSS is a reliable and validated questionnaire measuring three components of burnout. Leiter and Maslach explain that the emotional exhaustion (EE) items assess the level of emotional resources needed to sustain engagement at work.[13] The depersonalization (DP) items tap the ways in which people typically attempt to cope with interpersonal challenges encountered

---

12. For those interested in the development of the PAI and NAI, please see Malcolm et al., "Measuring Ministry-Specific Stress." See also Malcolm et al., "Complexity of Assessing."

13. Leiter and Maslach, "Latent Burnout Profiles."

in working with difficult people or on difficult tasks, and the personal accomplishment (PA) items focus on "the core self-evaluation people make regarding the value of their work and the quality of their contribution."[14] Norms have been established for the EE, DP, and PA scores, with low, average, or high range scores defined in the MBI manual. Together, the HSS subscale scores fall on a continuum from engagement (low EE and DP, and high PA) at one end of the spectrum to burnout (low PA, high EE and DP) at the other end of the spectrum.

Positive and Negative Aspects of Ministry-Life Inventories (PAI and NAI)

The PAI and NAI are a pair of questionnaires that are unique in providing information about twenty-nine aspects of ministry life. The PAI gathers data about seventeen "potentially positive" aspects of ministry life, while the NAI assesses twelve "potentially negative" aspects. Table 2 lists the PAI aspects and a sample item from each aspect, and table 2 lists the NAI aspects and sample items.

---

14. Leiter and Maslach, "Latent Burnout Profiles," 91.

Table 2. PAI Factors and Sample Items

	PAI FACTOR	SAMPLE ITEM
P1	Creative Initiative	Being open to trying new things
P2	Personal Spirituality	Integrating my personal spirituality with my ministry
P3	Personal Prayer	Spending time apart with God in prayer
P4	Leadership	Guiding a community
P5	Administration	Solving administrative problems
P6	Pastoral-Care Practices	Providing spiritual guidance
P7	Teaching	Facilitating small-group study
P8	Sharing the Gospel	Having opportunities to share my faith
P9	Fostering Faith Development	Seeing someone take on a passion and grow it
P10	Vocational Calling	Knowing that I am where God called me to be
P11	Social Responsibilities	Greeting newcomers
P12	Ongoing Learning	Having time to devote to study
P13	Building Work Relationships	Being valued and respected for my gifts and skills
P14	Time & Diversity of Tasks	Flexibility to organize my time
P15	Community Worship	Planning the worship portion of a service
P16	Liturgy	Immersing myself in liturgical life
P17	Preaching	Preparing a sermon

Table 3. NAI Factors and Sample Items

	NAI FACTOR	SAMPLE ITEM
N1	Role & Responsibility Pressure	The expectation that I be competent at a high number of different roles, many of which require very different skill sets
N2	Work Relationship Challenges	Absence of support from/among colleagues
N3	Challenges to Personal Spirituality	Going through a personal spiritual crisis
N4	Barriers to Personal Prayer Practices	Not enough time to spend in prayer and other spiritual disciplines
N5	Leading through Change and Controversy	Feeling torn between opposing factions among those to whom I minister
N6	Pastoral-Care Challenges	Responding to crises
N7	Boundaries	Continually having to be available to others
N8	Perceived-Expectations Strain	Being judged by a more stringent set of standards than those who are not in ministry
N9	Family vs. Ministry Conflict	Conflict between the needs of those to whom I minister and the needs of my family
N10	Time & Workload Strain	Being stretched too thinly over a wide range of tasks and projects
N11	Financial Challenges	Financial strain in the church/ministry I'm leading
N12	Preaching Challenges	Preparing a sermon

The PAI and NAI ask ministry workers to rate these aspects of their ministry life in terms of both (positive or negative) intensity and the frequency with which the aspects occur. We are not aware of any other measurement tools that use both intensity and frequency ratings in this way, and our research has shown that the impact of each aspect on an individual's overall stress and satisfaction levels is related not only to differences in how strongly positive or negative a given aspect is perceived to be but also how often the aspect is in play.[15] For example, a person might strongly value opportunities to provide spiritual care to those who are going through a difficult life transition or illness and thus rate it as a highly positive aspect of their ministry life. However, if they rarely have opportunities to engage in pastoral caregiving, the absence of these rewarding interactions might erode rather than build satisfaction. Neither positive intensity nor frequency alone sustain engagement, nor can negative intensity or frequency alone determine burnout.

Participants' intensity ratings (rated from zero [not at all] to four [very strongly]) and frequency ratings (rated from zero [never] to four [continually]) on the PAI and NAI are scored in such a way that each aspect of ministry life is placed into one of four quadrants, as shown on the graph in figure 1. For example, if "preaching" received a positive-intensity rating of three and a frequency rating of three, it would fall into the upper-right quadrant of high frequency–high intensity.

Figure 1. Frequency/Intensity Quadrant Model

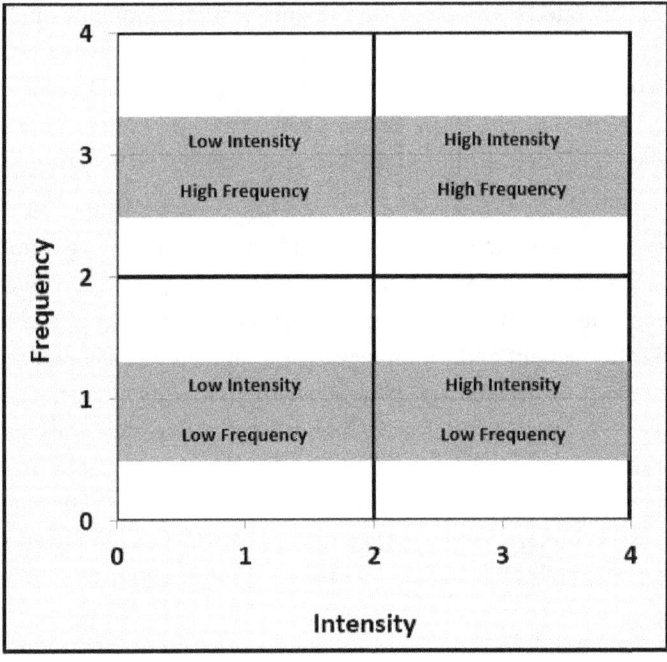

---

15. Malcolm et al., "Measuring Ministry-Specific Stress." See also Malcolm et al., "Complexity of Assessing."

The most pertinent findings from our earlier research are as follows:

1. Aspects rated by participants as high frequency–high intensity on the PAI (top-right quadrant in the figure above) have been named "core satisfiers," because they are associated with indices of engagement on the HSS (low EE and DP, and high PA).

2. Aspects that fall into any of the other three PAI quadrants are surprisingly associated with one or more indices of burnout on the HSS. To contextualize, when administrative tasks are rated as highly frequent and highly positive, "administration" operates as a core satisfier and is associated with indices of engagement. In contrast, when administrative tasks are rated as highly frequent but not very positive, they become a secondary stressor and are associated with indices of burnout (i.e., decreased PA, and higher EE and DP). We have theorized that these aspects are operating like the hindrances described by Crawford et al.—job demands experienced as obstacles to achieving work-related goals.[16]

3. Aspects rated by research participants as high frequency–high intensity on the NAI have been named "core stressors" because they are associated with HSS indices of burnout (high EE and DP, and depleted PA). For example, "time & workload strain" becomes a core stressor when it is rated as both highly frequent and highly negative.

4. Aspects that fall in either of the low-intensity quadrants on the NAI are in fact associated with indices of engagement.[17] To contextualize, establishing and navigating interpersonal boundaries are an ongoing reality in ministry life. When this aspect of ministry life is rated as highly frequent and highly negative, it operates as a core stressor. In contrast, if "boundaries" is rated as highly frequent but not intensely negative, it is associated with higher PA and operates as a satisfaction booster. Aspects of ministry life that are low in frequency and low in negative intensity are associated with decreased EE and DP and operate as stress buffers. We have therefore theorized, in keeping with Crawford and colleagues' work,[18] that aspects rated as satisfaction boosters

16. Crawford et al., "Linking Job Demands."

17. The low-frequency, high-negative-intensity quadrant is the only exception to this pattern, in that it is not significantly associated with any of the HSS subscales, making it neutral in effect.

18. Crawford et al., "Linking Job Demands."

and stress buffers are operating as challenges: work-related demands that are experienced as difficult but manageable job requirements.

5. Bringing together the PAI and NAI quadrants, we are able to identify "negative" and "positive" quadrants. The negative quadrants include secondary stressors, irritants, satisfaction eroders (all from the PAI), and core stressors (from the NAI). Participants' scores from these quadrants are averaged together to form a "stress score" consisting of the quadrant scores that have negative effects on well-being or are associated with indices of burnout. The positive quadrants include core satisfiers (from the PAI), satisfaction boosters, and stress buffers (from the NAI). These are also averaged together to provide a "satisfaction score" based on the quadrant scores that have positive effects on well-being or are associated with indices of engagement.

Equipped with these measures and our four-quadrant model, we set out in search of answers to a set of exploratory questions regarding MV ministry.

Research question 1: Are there marked differences between MV and UV ministry workers in the patterns of stress and burnout or satisfaction and engagement they report?

Much of the work a pastor does is invisible to those who attend church services, especially if they are not involved as volunteers, have not needed pastoral care, or have never sought out conversations with the pastor about their spiritual questions. One of our assumptions was that the invisibility of much ministry work is further amplified when individuals divide their time between two or more work settings. UV ministry workers may also lack appreciation for MV ministry workers. Peterson and Samushonga both comment that MV ministry is at times considered inferior to full-time ministry, because MV ministry workers are thought either to lack the skills needed to "succeed" in ministry or to have failed spiritually.[19] In the first instance, it is assumed that if MV ministry workers were better at their vocation, more people would attend their church and contribute financially, and the pastor would then be able to dedicate themself to full-time ministry. In the latter case, it is assumed that if the MV ministry workers had more faith, they would not have resorted to supporting themselves with work outside the church, and that this is the reason their ministry is not being blessed by God with financial contributions.

---

19. Peterson, "Working Priests." See also Samushonga, "Theological Reflection."

Neither of these are defensible arguments, and we take the stance that there are both benefits and costs associated with choosing to organize one's work life around two or more places of work. Among the benefits of MV ministry cited by Jones, Peterson, and Samushonga are the advantages of spending regular hours in work that is similar to the work church members are engaged in, sharing responsibility equitably with laity who understand and embrace the tasks involved in being members of a church together, financial independence from fluctuating church finances, and engaging in a holistic missional life in which the pastor's ministry encompasses their life both in and outside the church.[20] Other benefits have been explored in other chapters of this text.

Of course, MV ministry also has unique downsides. Based on his own experiences and his review of the literature, Samushonga points out that dividing one's work between two vocations adds to the pressure of ministry.[21] This pressure is due to the mental and emotional transitions involved in moving from one form of work to another, and to the possibility that the two (or more) types of work require more hours of work than one full-time position. In the same publication, Samushonga also notes that organizing one's work life around two or more work contexts requires that a person be especially effective in managing their time, particularly if they are to find a healthy work-life balance, preserving quality time for their family and for rest.[22]

Given the anecdotal evidence of both positive and negative differences between MV and UV ministry, our initial analysis compared the data provided by forty-one UV individuals with the data provided by sixty-one MV participants. Because the sixty-one MV participants included thirty-two individuals interviewed by the CMMP and twenty-nine non-CMMP MV ministry workers, we decided to treat the CMMP and non-CMMP MV participants as two separate groups. We could have limited our comparisons to the UV and thirty-two CMMP MV participants, but we chose to include the other group of MV ministry workers in order to compare the CMMP participants' responses with the responses of those who did not know we were interested in their vocational status, and to compare both MV groups' responses to those of UV ministry workers.

20. Jones, "Liturgy"; Peterson, "Working Priests"; Samushonga, "Theological Reflection."
21. Samushonga, "Theological Reflection," 76.
22. Samushonga, "Theological Reflection," 76.

HSS Profiles

Table 4 shows the means and standard deviations for the HSS comparisons of these three groups. Many statistical analyses rely on mean scores (the average obtained by adding all the values in a data set and then dividing it by the number of values in the data set). In this vein, the distance or range of scores around the mean, known as the standard deviation, becomes essential. The higher the standard deviation, the more spread out the data points. These values are then used to calculate whether group means differ from one another (with the critical assumption of approximately equal standard deviations). Our initial comparison between the groups revealed that UV, CMMP MV, and non-CMMP MV did not significantly differ from one another in their mean HSS scores. In other words, all groups were equal in their average levels of EE, DP, and PA.

Importantly, table 4 also includes mean norms provided in the MBI manual; regardless of whether ministry workers were MV or UV, their EE and PA scores were largely comparable to those reported by other human-service professions like teachers, police officers, social workers, etc. However, DP scores for non-CMMP MV and UV were significantly lower than that of other human-service professionals (based on known MBI norms). We do not currently have a hypothesis for this difference; future research would be needed to explore this further.

Table 4. Descriptive HSS Results

Means (SDs)	Emotional Exhaustion	Depersonalization	Personal Accomplishment
MBI Norms	21.42 (11.5)	8.11 (6.15)	36.43 (7.00)
All (n = 102)	20.35 (11.48)	5.90 (5.46)	34.46 (6.14)
CMMP MV (n = 32)	18.22 (11.86)	6.31 (5.86)	33.00 (6.13)
Non-CMMP MV (n = 29)	22.96 (12.15)	5.55 (4.71)	35.69 (6.03)
UV (n = 41)	20.17 (10.59)	5.83 (5.73)	34.73 (6.14)

Of note, Leiter and Maslach report the results of research based on two large studies of health-services staff that allowed them to identify the different profiles that can be derived from the MBI.[23] They show that engaged workers enjoy low levels of EE and DP and a strong sense of PA. Workers experiencing professional burnout suffer from high levels of EE and DP as well as a depleted sense of PA, while those approaching burnout report high levels of EE and DP but retain average or high levels of PA. Table 5 shows the percentage of participants in each group who reported these MBI profiles. Interestingly, the CMMP MV participants were more likely than either the UV or non-CMMP MV participants to report both engaged and burnout MBI profiles, and less likely to report scores suggesting that they were approaching burnout. It appears, then, that the CMMP ministry workers were more likely than the comparison groups to be experiencing ministry life either at the engaged or burned-out extremes of the engagement/burnout spectrum.

Table 5. HSS Profile Comparison

	UV (n = 41)	CMMP MV (n = 32)	Non-CMMP MV (n = 29)
Engaged	10 percent	16 percent	7 percent
Approaching Burnout[24]	10 percent	0 percent	7 percent
Burnout	7 percent	22 percent	3 percent

PAI and NAI Differences

We were surprised not to see any significant differences in levels of satisfaction, stress, or indices of burnout when comparing MV and UV participants. As we looked at the CMMP interview transcripts, participants spoke about experiences that echoed the aspects captured by the PAI and NAI items. This made us wonder if, despite the overall mean levels of stress and satisfaction being comparable, the sources of stress might differ for people

23. Leiter and Maslach, "Latent Burnout Profiles."

24. Leiter and Maslach found this profile strongly present in one of their studies, and established that it has the downsides of both high EE and high DP subscale scores rather than the downsides of a high score on only one of the subscales. They have not reported further investigations of this profile, however, so until further research is carried out, only tentative conclusions can be drawn from the fact that UV and non-CMMP MV participants but no CMMP participants had this profile.

in MV contexts compared to those in the UV group. Consequently, we decided to compare our MV and UV participants to see if there were marked differences in the specific aspects most often rated as core satisfiers and stressors. For example, we wondered if, due to their multiple jobs, MV ministry workers would be more likely to experience "time & workload strain" as a core stressor. Similarly, we wondered if there would be aspects that are less likely to be core satisfiers because they are not as frequently available to be enjoyed. While there were some minor differences in the rankings of core satisfiers and core stressors, we found no compelling support for the argument that the sources of satisfaction and stress differ depending on whether a person is involved in UV or MV ministry.

Research question 2: Is it possible that there are demographic factors masking the differences between UV and MV ministry workers?

The next step in our analysis was to address the possibility that some of the demographic factors were masking group differences. For example, several researchers have reported gender differences in HSS scores, and it is possible that these gender differences were obscuring differences between UV and MV ministry workers in their experience of ministry life.[25] Matching is a way to handle potentially confounding variables.[26] To be specific, since gender itself does not cause burnout, matching the UV and MV groups in the number of men and women in each group equalizes any gender effect on HSS scores. Unfortunately, to our knowledge, no research has previously compared UV and MV participants, so it was difficult to know which factors to consider. However, the possible impact of gender is noteworthy, as is the evidence in our previous research that ordination status (ordained vs non-ordained) and differences in participants' years of experience have an impact on the quality of ministry life in general.[27] To equalize these potentially confounding demographic factors, we matched a group of UV participants to the CMMP MV group based on gender, ordination status, and years of experience. Once again, we found no significant differences. On average, the CMMP MV and matched UV ministry workers were comparable in their HSS, PAI, and NAI scores. It is possible, then, that even though there are real differences between *individual* MV and UV

---

25. Adekola, "Gender Differences." See also Bakker et al., "Validation"; Markus et al., "Gender Differences"; and Purvanova and Muros, "Gender Differences in Burnout."

26. Graaf et al., "Matching."

27. Malcolm et al., "Complexity of Assessing."

ministry workers' experience of ministry life, there are no overall *group* differences that are exclusively due to vocational status (i.e., UV vs. MV).

Future Research Recommendations Arising from Our First Two Research Questions

Even though this initial exploration of potential differences did not uncover statistically significant differences in experiences of satisfaction and stress, further exploration between and within these two frameworks for Christian ministry is needed given the strong anecdotal report from people in both MV and UV settings that the two types of work have distinct and unique stressors and satisfiers. Research within each framework would further illuminate the internal forces within MV and UV that are sustaining wellness and contributing to the risk of burnout for people engaged in such ministry.

Despite the surprising lack of differences in our sample of UV and MV ministry workers, it would be premature to draw the conclusion that there are no differences between UV and MV ministry workers in these two types of ministry life. Our results are based on an exploratory investigation with a small sample of participants, and given that this is a new area within the larger research field of clergy wellness and burnout, we encourage further research with HSS, PAI, and NAI data collected from a larger number of participants. In addition, we encourage research that builds on the work that has already been carried out by graduate students, especially if that research is expanded to include UV and MV comparison groups and with the intent to submit the results for publication in peer-reviewed social-science journals.

It was disappointing to find so little peer-reviewed empirical research about MV ministry. Part of what troubles us is that demographic information about vocational status (i.e., UV vs. MV) is not usually included in the description of participants, which makes it impossible to know how many of the studies on clergy wellness and burnout include both UV and MV participants, and how the results might have differed if such information had been collected and analyzed separately for comparison purposes. Even our own previous research is based on data collected from an unknown combination of MV and UV ministry workers.[28] In fact, as far as we know, no clergy-wellness researchers have previously published a study that looks

---

28. Malcolm et al., "Measuring Ministry-Specific Stress."

at the relevance of vocational status. This stands as a surprising contradiction to the deeply held anecdotal convictions that UV and MV ministry are at least qualitatively different experiences for the individuals engaged in ministry.

Research question 3: Are there differences *within* the CMMP MV group that are important in and of themselves or that might explain why we found no significant differences between MV and UV participants?

If the key difference is not between UV and MV ministry, then where does the difference lie? Considering the absence of significant or meaningful differences, we began to wonder if the differences might be *within* MV ministry rather than between MV and UV ministry. Thus, we took a closer look at the questions asked and the themes identified in the qualitative component of the CMMP research. In examining the narrative data, we saw a potential difference that seemed highly relevant to our empirical investigation. Many participants explicitly stated whether or not they would choose to remain in MV ministry when asked, "If you could make your work life exactly what you wanted, would you continue to divide your work the way it is, or would you make substantial changes?" Some participants conveyed the impression that they had always known that MV ministry was their calling; some expressed a desire to switch to UV ministry; and some spoke of originally wanting to switch but having come to the conclusion that their gifts and personality have made MV ministry such a good fit for them that they would not now accept an invitation to switch to UV ministry. We pulled narrative data that represented each participant's stance on whether they would leave MV ministry or choose to stay if given the opportunity. These interview excerpts were then read separately by two team members, and the CMMP participants were categorized either as "choose to leave" or "choose to stay" in MV ministry. There was rater agreement for twenty-nine of the thirty-two interview excerpts, and the three that were rated differently were discussed until agreement was reached. Based on this process, nine CMMP participants were identified as individuals who would leave MV ministry if given the option of a UV position, and twenty-one were categorized as individuals who would stay in MV ministry even if given the option of a UV position. Two participants were excluded from the subsequent analysis because both raters agreed that it was impossible to tell from the interview excerpts whether they would choose to leave MV ministry or would stay if given the option of a UV ministry position.

PART 1 | CANADIAN MULTIVOCATIONAL MINISTRY PROJECT

The choose-to-stay and choose-to-leave participants' data was then analyzed, yielding the following results (shown in figure 2): Participants who would choose to leave reported statistically higher average levels of emotional exhaustion and depersonalization on the HSS. Both groups reported similar average levels of personal achievement.

Figure 2. Mean HSS Subscale Scores for Choose-to-Leave versus Choose-to-Stay CMMP Participants

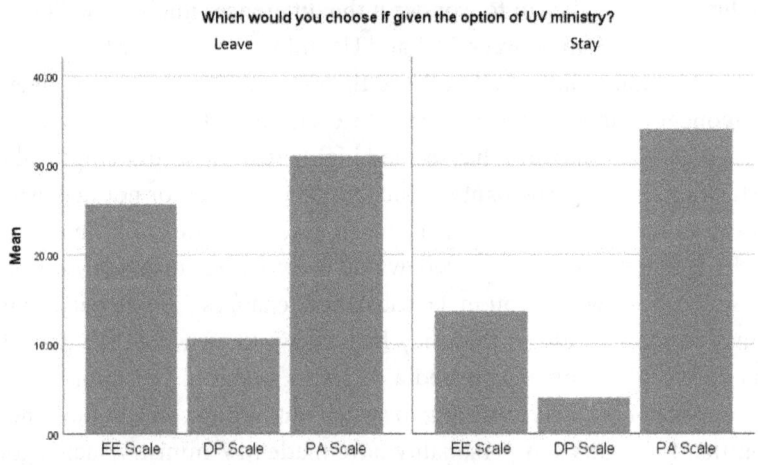

In looking at quadrant scores from the PAI, choose-to-leave participants reported fewer core satisfiers than participants who would choose to stay, whereas the two groups were similar in average levels of secondary stressors (see figure 3). On the NAI, the two groups reported similar levels of core stressors.

Figure 3. Mean Core-Satisfier Percentage Scores for Choose-to-Leave versus Choose-to-Stay CMMP Participants

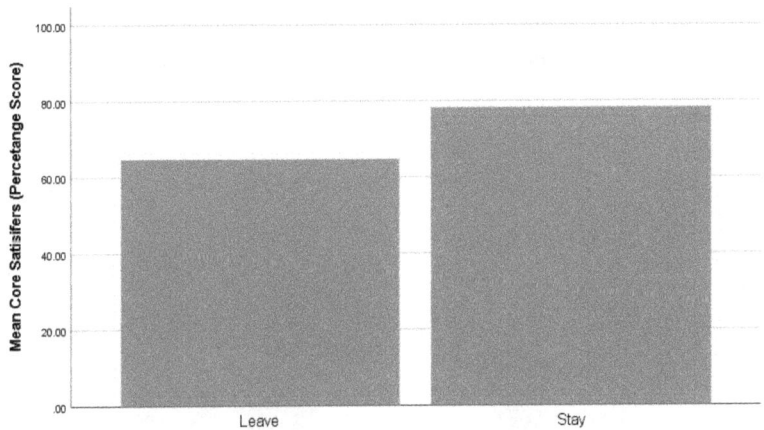

We then combined all the "negative" quadrants, followed by combining all the "positive" quadrants. These were averaged together to create overall satisfaction and stress scores. Interestingly, the choose-to-leave participants had significantly lower satisfaction scores and significantly higher stress scores (see figure 4) than the choose-to-stay participants. We also wondered whether there were differences regarding the ratio of the satisfaction-to-stress score. Those who chose to stay had a (marginally) significantly higher satisfaction-to-stress ratio (see figure 4) than those who would choose to leave. In other words, choose-to-stay participants had higher overall satisfaction scores relative to overall stress scores than did choose-to-leave participants.

Figure 4. Mean Satisfaction Scores, Stress Scores, and Satisfaction-Stress Ratio Scores for Choose-to-Leave versus Choose-to-Stay CMMP Participants

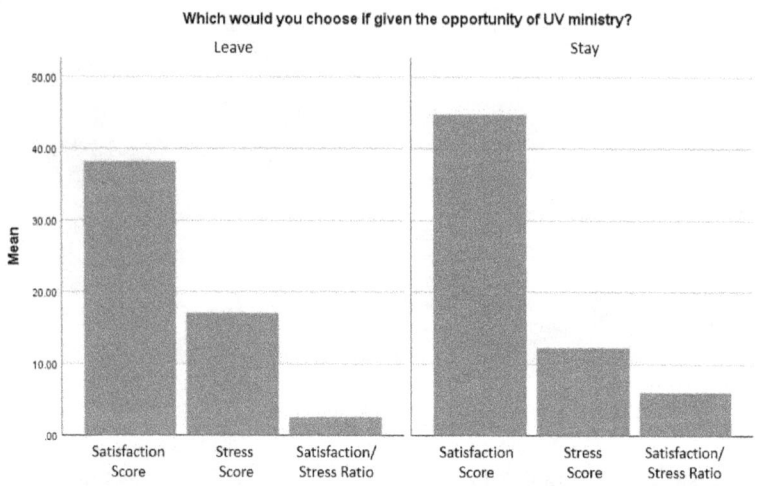

Returning to differences between the UV, CMMP MV, and non-CMMP MV participants, what stood out regarding the HSS subscale scores was that the CMMP participants were more likely than the comparison groups to be experiencing ministry life either from the engaged or the burned-out extremes of the engagement/burnout spectrum. Here, in comparing the CMMP choose-to-stay and choose-to-leave subgroups, we see the possibility that this difference is due to the fact that none of the CMMP participants with "engaged" profiles were among the choose-to-leave group, and that the percentage of participants experiencing burnout is noticeably higher among the choose-to-leave group (table 6). This suggests that workers who have taken up or continued in MV ministry by choice are more likely to report indices of engagement, while those who would leave MV ministry if they could do so are more likely to report symptoms of burnout. Furthermore, there were no participants in this sample whose responses were in the "approaching-burnout" category, reinforcing our conjecture that choice plays a crucial role in the experience of MV ministry life.

Table 6. CMMP HSS Profiles

	Choose-to-Stay	Choose-to-Leave
Engaged	16 percent	0 percent
Approaching Burnout	0 percent	0 percent
Burnout	6 percent	16 percent

Further differences were evident when we looked at the core satisfiers and core stressors of the two groups. Our first observation is that the choose-to-stay CMMP participants gave stronger ratings on the PAI, with the result that more than 90 percent of this group were experiencing five of the PAI aspects as core satisfiers. Table 7 shows that in this, they are like the matched UV participants, of whom more than 90 percent were experiencing four of the PAI aspects as core satisfiers. In contrast, the choose-to-leave CMMP MV participants had lower PAI ratings, such that only 80–89 percent rated three aspects as core satisfiers, and only 70–79 percent rated two more aspects as core satisfiers. None of the potentially positive aspects were experienced as core satisfiers by more than 90 percent of the choose-to-leave group. This is in keeping with the lower overall-satisfaction scores that the choose-to-leave group was experiencing.

Table 7. CMMP Top Five Core Satisfiers

	32 Matched UV	Choose-to-Stay	Choose-to-Leave
90–100 percent	Vocational Calling Building Work Relationships Study & Learning Time & Diversity of Tasks	Personal Spirituality Building Work Relationships Vocational Calling Preaching Creative Initiative	
80–89 percent			Personal Spirituality Vocational Calling Study & Learning
70–79 percent			Social Responsibilities Building Work Relationships

Our second observation was that the opposite pattern occurred for the NAI; the choose-to-leave CMMP participants gave stronger ratings for the NAI aspects, such that four of the aspects ("time & workload strain," "barriers to personal prayer," "challenges to personal spirituality," and "leading through change & controversy") were rated as core stressors by more than 50 percent of this group. These aspects were also among the most frequent aspects rated as core stressors by the choose-to-stay group but were selected by less than 50 percent of the group. Table 8 shows that in this respect, the choose-to-stay group are again more like the matched UV group.

Table 8. CMMP Top Five Core Stressors

	32 Matched UV	Choose-to-Stay	Choose-to-Leave
70–79 percent			Time & Workload Strain
60–69 percent			Barriers to Personal Prayer
50–59 percent			Challenges to Personal Spirituality Leading Through Change & Controversy
40–49 percent	Barriers to Personal Prayer Time & Workload Strain	Barriers to Personal Prayer Time & Workload Strain	
30–39 percent	Work Relationship Challenges Leading Through Change and & Controversy Boundaries	Work Relationship Challenges Challenges to Personal Spirituality Leading Through Change & Controversy	Role Expectations & Responsibilities Boundaries Perceived Expectations Strain

Future Research Recommendations Arising from Our Third Research Question

Replicating this research with a larger sample of MV ministry workers would be an important way to confirm possible trends or amplify differences that may be too small to see with a sample size of only thirty-two participants. It also seems clear to us that further qualitative research regarding choosing to stay versus leaving if given the option of UV ministry could yield fruitful insights and a deeper understanding of MV ministry experiences.

The pattern of differences that emerged from our comparison between the choose-to-stay and choose-to-leave MV ministry groups is quite intriguing and leads us to wonder if similar differences would also be found among UV ministry workers. Is it possible that there are individuals in UV ministry who would switch to MV ministry if they had the option to do so, or who have remained in UV ministry despite being unfulfilled because they do not have the training, skills, or experience that would permit a financially feasible career change?

Conclusion

Our first research question led us to carry out a set of exploratory tests for differences in our data between UV, CMMP MV, and non-CMMP MV ministry workers in the patterns of stress and burnout or satisfaction and engagement they report. We found no statistically significant differences in their HSS or PAI and NAI quadrant scores, and no outstanding patterns of difference in aspects rated as core satisfiers or stressors. The only potentially meaningful difference found was that the CMMP MV participants were more likely than the UV or non-CMMP MV participants to report scores at the extremes of the engagement/burnout spectrum. Our second research question positioned us to test for differences between a matched group of thirty-two UV and the thirty-two CMMP MV individuals. Again, no statistically significant or meaningful differences were found.

Our third research question focused on understanding differences observed within the CMMP MV group between those who would choose to leave MV ministry if a UV position were to become available to them and those who would choose to stay in MV ministry even if a UV position were offered. Statistically, the choose-to-leave group was more likely to report symptoms of burnout and fewer core satisfiers on the PAI. The differences in rating between these two groups also resulted in a higher satisfaction-to-stress ratio for the choose-to-stay group, a ratio we believe is needed to maintain vocational wellness and to consistently enjoy positive engagement in the work of ministry.

We had earlier noted a tendency among CMMP participants to be experiencing ministry life either from the engaged or burnout extremes of the engagement/burnout spectrum. We saw that none of the choose-to-leave participants had engaged profiles, and while there were only one or two individuals in each group who reported scores consistent with a burnout profile, the statistical impact of this on a group of nine is much stronger than the impact on a group of twenty-one participants. Comparing core-satisfier and core-stressor ratings also revealed differences. The choose-to-stay group gave stronger PAI ratings, while the choose-to-leave group gave stronger NAI ratings, with the result that the choose-to-stay group's ratings were more like the ratings made by the matched UV group than those of the choose-to-leave group.

We expected to find statistically significant differences in the experiences of satisfaction and stress of people in MV ministry when compared to those in UV ministry, and were surprised not to find them in either HSS or PAI/NAI data. What this suggests to us is that MV ministry is inherently no more nor less satisfying or stressful than UV ministry. It also suggests that the reality of anecdotal convictions about differences probably resides in contextual and situational differences and not in group membership. For example, not everyone working in an MV context has intentionally chosen this situation for themselves, and what does seem to have a significant effect on experiences of satisfaction and stress for people engaged in MV ministry is whether they have chosen this form of ministry out of a sense of vocational calling and fit, or whether have found themselves in MV ministry out of financial necessity or because other circumstances require it of them.

The CMMP participants who said they had taken up or were continuing in MV ministry by choice were more likely to be enjoying a sustained level of positive engagement with their work. In contrast, those who said they would leave MV ministry if they could do so were more likely to be experiencing the taxing effects of the emotional work involved and struggling to cope with the inevitable interpersonal challenges of working with difficult people or on difficult tasks. Furthermore, there were no participants in this sample whose responses fell in the "approaching-burnout" category, reinforcing our conjecture that choice plays a pivotal role in the experience of MV ministry life.

Satisfaction and stress in ministry are complex realities, whether one is working in a UV or an MV context. Given our findings that MV ministry may be as satisfying *and* as stressful as UV ministry, it seems to us that it is important to validate MV ministry as a choice on equal footing with UV ministry. We see no clear patterns that suggest MV ministry is inherently more difficult or stressful than "normative" UV ministry, and we do see that profound satisfaction is present for the MV ministry workers who participated in our research. There is much to be said about the richness of MV work, and it seems to us that the most important factor in MV well-being is the individual worker's perception of MV ministry as a deliberate and desired choice rather than a necessity or suboptimal option. This suggests to us that in the same way individuals and communities of faith discern a calling to traditional UV ministry, MV ministry ought to be seen and celebrated as a call discerned by the individual and their community.

Questions for Reflection

1. If you had the opportunity to work in this new field of research, what research questions would you want to investigate? How might that help the church and both UV and MV ministry workers accurately appreciate the blessings of MV ministry and respect the challenges involved?

2. From your own experiences, what do you make of the differences between the choose-to-stay and choose-to-leave MV ministry groups? What role have personal choice and financial constraints played in your vocational decision-making?

3. Given our findings that the experiences of satisfaction and stress are similar between (choose-to-stay) MV and UV ministry workers, why do you think MV ministry is so often seen as a suboptimal form of ministry work? Why might it be important to change this perception?

PART 1 | CANADIAN MULTIVOCATIONAL MINISTRY PROJECT

Bibliography

Adekola, Bola. "Gender Differences in the Experience of Work Burnout among University Staff." *African Journal of Business Management* 4 (2010) 886–89. https://academicjournals.org/journal/AJBM/article-abstract/E64B91023543.

Bakker, Arnold B., et al. "Validation of the Maslach Burnout Inventory—General Survey: An Internet Study." *Anxiety, Stress and Coping* 15 (2002) 245–60. https://doi.org/10.1080/1061580021000020716.

Crawford, Eean R., et al. "Linking Job Demands and Resources to Employee Engagement and Burnout: A Theoretical Extension and Meta-Analytic Test." *Journal of Applied Psychology* 95 (2010) 834–48. https://doi.org/10.1037/a0019364.

Freudenberger, H. J., and G. Richelson. *Burnout: The High Cost of High Achievement*. Garden City, NY: Doubleday, 1980.

Graaf, Michiel A. de, et al. "Matching, an Appealing Method to Avoid Confounding?" *Nephron–Clinical Practice* 118 (2011) 315–18. https://doi.org/10.1159/000323136.

Jones, Sandra K. "Liturgy, Pastoral Ministry, and the Bivocational Pastor." *Liturgy* 32 (2017) 32–39. https://doi.org/10.1080/0458063X.2017.1343049.

Leiter, Michael P., and Christina Maslach. "Latent Burnout Profiles: A New Approach to Understanding the Burnout Experience." *Burnout Research* 3 (2016) 89–100. https://doi.org/10.1016/j.burn.2016.09.001.

Malcolm, Wanda M., et al. "The Complexity of Assessing Ministry-Specific Satisfaction and Stress." *Journal of Psychology and Theology* (2021) 1–20. https://doi.org/10.1177/00916471211021921.

Malcolm, Wanda M., et al. "Measuring Ministry-Specific Stress and Satisfaction: The Psychometric Properties of the Positive and Negative Aspects Inventories." *Journal of Psychology and Theology* 47 (2019) 313–27. https://doi.org/10.1177/0091647119837018.

Markus, Canazei, et al. "Gender Differences in Different Dimensions of Common Burnout Symptoms in a Group of Clinical Burnout Patients" *Neuropsychiatry* 8 (2018) 1967–76. https://www.jneuropsychiatry.org/peer-review/gender-differences-in-different-dimensions-of-common-burnout-symptoms-in-a-group-of-clinical-burnout-patients-12860.html.

Maslach, Christina, et al. *Maslach Burnout Inventory Manual*. 4th ed. N.p., 1996. https://www.mindgarden.com/maslach-burnout-inventory-mbi/685-mbi-manual.html

Mikail, Sam. "Professional Self Care." Webinar. Barbara Wand Symposium, College of Psychologists of Ontario, September 15, 2020.

Moeller, Julia, et al. "Highly Engaged but Burned out: Intra-Individual Profiles in the US Workforce." *Career Development International* 23 (2018) 86–105. https://doi.org/10.1108/CDI-12-2016-0215.

Nerstad, Christina G. L., et al. "Can Engagement Go Awry and Lead to Burnout? The Moderating Role of the Perceived Motivational Climate." *International Journal of Environmental Research and Public Health* 16 (2019). https://doi.org/10.3390/ijerph16111979.

Perry, Samuel L., and Cyrus Schleifer. "Are Bivocational Clergy Becoming the New Normal? An Analysis of the Current Population Survey, 1996–2017." *Journal for the Scientific Study of Religion* 58 (2019) 513–25. https://doi.org/10.1111/jssr.12593.

Peterson, Aaron. "Working Priests: Improving the Care for Vineyard Bivocational Pastors." DMin diss., George Fox University, 2018. https://digitalcommons.georgefox.edu/dmin/254/.

Purvanova, Radostina K., and John P. Muros. "Gender Differences in Burnout: A Meta-Analysis." *Journal of Vocational Behavior* 77 (2010) 168–85. https://doi.org/10.1016/j.jvb.2010.04.006.

Samushonga, Hartness M. "A Theological Reflection of Bivocational Pastoral Ministry: A Personal Reflective Account of a Decade of Bivocational Ministry Practice Experience." *Practical Theology* 12 (2019) 66–80. https://doi.org/10.1080/1756073X.2019.1575040.

Part 2

Biblical and Theological Reflections on Tentmaking

3

What Multivocational Ministers Can Learn from Paul's Tentmaking Experience

Narry F. Santos

THE APOSTLE PAUL'S TENTMAKING experience offers valuable insights to twenty-first-century multivocational ministers. To unearth such insights, this chapter will explore Paul's tentmaking experience as revealed in the book of Acts and some of the Pauline letters. Particularly, we will look at two aspects of his life and ministry: (1) his self-identity as Paul the tentmaker, why he engaged in his trade, and how it relates to his mission; and (2) key descriptions of (and lessons from) his toil and labor (i.e., shared and team ministry, use of the workshop as a social venue for mission, and willingness to suffer as a tentmaker and missionary). At the end of the chapter, I (as a multivocational minister myself) will briefly offer some reflections on Paul's tentmaking experience and share what multivocational ministers can learn from Paul in light of the current Canadian and Western society.

Apostle Paul's Identity as Tentmaker

Paul's call as apostle has been widely recognized and adequately discussed.[1] However, a key aspect of Paul's identity that has been occasionally affirmed and sporadically researched is Paul the tentmaker. Scholars pay

---

1. Dunn, *Theology of Paul*; Picirilli, *Paul the Apostle*; Schnelle, *Apostle Paul*; Bruce, *Paul*.

scant attention to Paul's tentmaking because they regard it as a peripheral matter.[2] However, Adolf Deismann considers the apostle as "Paul the tentmaker," who had "worked at his trade for wages which were the economic basis of his existence."[3] Ronald Hock also argues that Paul's being a tentmaker was central to his life, if not forming "part of his self-understanding as an apostle."[4] Others agree that Paul's toil as a tentmaker marked not only his apostolic self-identity but also his missionary activity.[5] In other words, Paul's tentmaking was integrated into his personal life, apostolic ministry, and mission to the gentiles more than is generally recognized among scholars.

Understanding Paul's Tentmaking Trade

That Paul was a tentmaker (*skenopoios*) occurs only once in the New Testament (Acts 18:3). Though it is possible for the tent cloth to come from woven goat's hair (*cilicium*), it seems more likely that Paul used leather to make tents.[6] The etymological meaning of *skenopoios* is "tentmaker," but the term probably meant "leather worker." Such leatherwork could have been intended not only for tents for patrons' use but also for booths, canopies, and awnings for city use.[7] Thus, "we can picture Paul sitting in his patron's workshops cutting and sewing leather to make tents (and probably other leather goods)."[8]

A key question that arises in light of Paul's identity as tentmaker is this: How did Paul learn his craft? New Testament scholars have presented three options, namely: (1) Paul could have learned his trade from his father as a child in Tarsus;[9] (2) Paul could have learned it as a student in Jerusalem under Gamaliel;[10] and (3) Paul could have learned it at some point after his

---

2. Tolmie, "Mission and the Workplace," 94.

3. Deismann, *Paul*, 48.

4. Tolmie, "Mission and the Workplace," 94. Tolmie's words.

5. Meeks, *First Urban Christians*, 9; Horrell, *Social Ethos*, 76; Meggitt, *Paul, Poverty and Survival*, 75–77.

6. Michealis, "*Skenopoios*," 39–94.

7. Throckmorton, "Tentmaker," 573; Thompson, "Trades and Occupations," 2092; Smith, "Tentmaker," 523.

8. Hock, "Workshop as Social Setting," 450.

9. Hock, *Social Context*, 24; Heyer, *Paul*, 30.

10. Polhill, *Paul and His Letters*, 9; Longnecker, *Acts*, 135; Barnett, "Tentmaking,"

conversion or call prior to his missionary travels.[11] Because of these different scholarly speculations, Todd Still contends that "it is now impossible to determine when, where, and from whom Paul learned his craft."[12] However, Paul being a tentmaker was in accordance with the custom that required every rabbi to have a trade in order to support themselves. As William Barclay argues, "Rabbis were not detached scholars and always knew what the life of the working man was like."[13]

So far, we have seen that Paul's self-understanding as an apostle was linked to his being a tentmaker, who worked with leather to make tents and other leather-related products. Paul's tentmaking trade, which he probably gained as a rabbinical student under Gamaliel, marked his apostolic self-identity and mission to the gentiles. Paul was not just Paul the apostle but also Paul the tentmaker—an aspect of his self-identity that was central to his life and ministry. Hock aptly captures the centrality of Paul's self-identity as apostle and tentmaker with these words:

> Far from being at the periphery of his life, Paul's tentmaking was actually central to it. More than any one of us has supposed, Paul was Paul the Tentmaker.... His trade was taken up in his apostolic self-understanding, so much so that when criticized for plying his trade, he came to understand himself as the apostle who offered the gospel free of charge.[14]

Why Paul Engaged in Tentmaking While Ministering

Having established that Paul the tentmaker is central to his apostolic self-identity and mission to the gentiles, it is now important to understand the reasons why Paul wanted to engage in tentmaking while he ministered. Why did he choose to become a tentmaker? This is a crucial question in light of the Lord's clear admonition that the laborer for God "deserves to be paid" (Luke 10:7b; cf. Matt 10:10b) and Paul's agreement to the Lord's commandment "that those who proclaim the gospel should get their living by the gospel" (1 Cor 9:14). Despite these rights, Paul still declared, "But I have

---

924; Bornkamm, *Paul*, 12; Bruce, *Paul*, 107–8, 220.
   11. Murphy-O'Connor, *Paul*, 86; Reisner, *Paul's Early Period*, 149.
   12. Still, "Did Paul Loathe," 785.
   13. Barclay, *Acts of the Apostles*, 135.
   14. Hock, *Social Context*, 67.

made no use of any of these rights" (1 Cor 9:15a). He kept a firm stance on tentmaking and offering the gospel free of charge in Corinth (1 Cor 9:18). This stance is also intriguing considering that Paul received gifts from the Macedonian churches during his ministry in Corinth (2 Cor 11:9) and from the Philippian church during his ministry in Thessalonica (Phil 4:16).

According to Peter Marshall, Paul gave three reasons for his refusal to accept a salary or a gift in addressing the Corinthians. These reasons are as follows: (1) Paul did not want to place an obstacle in the way of the gospel (1 Cor 9:12b); (2) he did not want to burden anyone (2 Cor 11:9, 12:13–14); and (3) he loved them (2 Cor 11:11, 12:15).[15] In addition, from the perspective of missiology, J. J. Kritzinger presents five reasons why Paul engaged in tentmaking and did not accept money for his ministry, namely: (1) Paul did not want to lay a burden on the congregations; (2) he did not want to be associated with preachers who misused their right to maintenance and became parasites; (3) he wanted to portray an example of manual labor to the congregations; (4) he wanted to reiterate the principle of giving as being better than receiving; and (5) he made sacrifices mainly from a missionary point of view in order to "become all things to all people, that I might by all means save some" (1 Cor 9:22b).[16]

There are many other reasons that scholars propose,[17] but here are six more plausible reasons. First, "plying a trade" was a normal practice among the Jews.[18] Second, Paul used his trade as a springboard for evangelism in the marketplace.[19] Third, he adopted a servant attitude in line with Jesus' command in Matt 20:28.[20] Fourth, he was reluctant to enter into a client relation within the framework of patronage with rich Christians.[21] Fifth, he made sure that the collection for Jerusalem was not misinterpreted as a collection for himself.[22] Sixth, he looked to open the door, especially for the

---

15. Marshall, *Enmity in Corinth*, 233.

16. Wessels ("Contextual Views on Paul," 14) translated these five reasons from Kritzinger's book (*Missionere Bediening*, 183–85).

17. See Wessels, "Contextual Views on Paul," 19, for a list of sixteen reasons at the conclusion of his article.

18. Hock, *Social Context*, 28.

19. Hock, "Paul's Tentmaking," 560.

20. Wolff, "Humility and Self-Denial," 145–50.

21. Marshall, *Enmity in Corinth*, 402; Witherington, *Paul Quest*, 128–29.

22. Agrell, *Work, Toil, and Sustenance*, 110–11.

poor,[23] so that people could enter the church whatever their socio-economic status and be saved.[24]

These various reasons cited above help explain why Paul chose to serve as both tentmaker and apostle, realizing that this dual self-identity could aid him to fulfill his mission from God—without putting hindrances to the gospel and without becoming a burden to anyone. Paul used his gifts (including his skills as a tentmaker) to be on mission with God wherever he went (e.g., workshops, homes, synagogues, halls) and whoever was with him (whether Jew or gentile, rich or poor, male or female). In short, Paul found meaning, purpose, and fulfillment as a tentmaker that led him to ply his trade as part of his holistic mission and to use it as a social venue for ministry whenever he had the opportunity.

Descriptions of Paul's Tentmaking Experience

Having seen Paul the apostle's self-identity as Paul the tentmaker and why he engaged in his trade in fulfilling God's mission for him, it is important to also look at the descriptions of (or lessons from) Paul's tentmaking experience. Three descriptions or lessons stand out, namely: (1) shared labor and team ministry; (2) use of the tentmaker's workshop as a social venue for connection and mission; and (3) willingness to suffer as a tentmaker and missionary.

Paul's Travel, Ministry, and Work with Others

Paul's letters and the book of Acts provide good evidence that wherever and whenever Paul was doing missionary preaching and teaching, Paul would be found in a workshop or working as a tentmaker.[25] In fact, in his missionary journeys, Paul traveled, ministered, and worked with others in a team. In his first missionary journey, Paul traveled with Barnabas (Acts 13:1—14:28). It is interesting that Paul commented about himself and Barnabas working together: "Or is it only Barnabas and I who have no rights to refrain from working for a living?" (1 Cor 9:6). This reference probably extends the

---

23. Deismann, *Paul*, 208.
24. Robbins, *Tapestry of Christian Discourse*, 87–88.
25. Hock, "Workshop as Social Setting," 439.

PART 2 | BIBLICAL AND THEOLOGICAL REFLECTIONS ON TENTMAKING

coverage back to their first missionary journey together,[26] which implies that Paul and Barnabas did not only travel and minister together but also worked together at certain times in their missionary journey.

In his second missionary journey, Paul had Silas and Timothy join him in Thessalonica (Acts 17:1–5; 1 Thess 1:1; 3:2, 6) and Corinth (Acts 18:5). Paul reminded the Thessalonians of the work that he and his missionary team did while ministering among them: "You remember our labor and toil, brothers and sisters; we worked night and day, so that we might not be a burden to any of you while we proclaimed to you the gospel of God" (1 Thess 2:9). Moreover, Paul asked the Corinthians to remember his team's difficult manual labor while doing the ministry among the believers: "And we grew weary from the work of our hands" (1 Cor 4:12). In Corinth, we also see the only reference to Paul as tentmaker (Acts 18:3a). Paul stayed and worked with Aquila and Priscilla, who were also tentmakers like Paul (Acts 18:3b) and who fled from Rome due to Claudius's order for all Jews to leave Italy (Acts 18:2). Just as we saw Paul's travel team minister and work during the first missionary journey, we again see Paul's missionary team do the same combination of ministry and manual labor in the second journey. Even when Paul intended to visit Corinth for a third time (2 Cor 12:14a), he clearly expressed that he would not be a burden to them (2 Cor 12:14b) and that he would "most gladly spend and be spent" for them (2 Cor 14:15a).

In his third missionary journey, Paul had Gaius and Aristarchus, his traveling companions from Macedonia (Acts 19:29), minister with him in Ephesus (Acts 19:23–41). In Paul's farewell address to the Ephesian leaders (Acts 20:17–35), he refreshed their memory regarding his hard work among them: "You know for yourselves that I worked with my own hands to support myself and my companions" (Acts 20:34). Even in his third journey, Paul continued to work as a tentmaker, even using the proceeds of his manual labor to support not just his needs but also those of his missionary team (Gaius and Aristarchus; Acts 19:23–41).

As we saw in the earlier section, Paul received support or gifts from the Philippian church and other Macedonian churches (Phil 4:16, 2 Cor 11:9). It is also probable that he was financially supported by wealthy Christians (like Lydia in Acts 16:14–15),[27] but Paul continued to work while he and his missionary teams proclaimed the gospel of God.[28] In fact, the members of

---

26. Hock, *Social Context*, 26.
27. Tolmie, "Mission and the Workplace," 98.
28. Onongha, "Tentmaking," 190.

his travel team also worked with their hands as they ministered with Paul. Thus, as is evident in his missionary journeys, Paul commonly practiced team and shared leadership, as he and co-missionaries traveled, ministered, and worked together.

Workshop as Paul's Social Venue for Connection and Mission

We have discussed the first description of Paul's tentmaking ministry: the sharing of the labor and mission with teams. The second description is that Paul employed the workshop as a social venue for connection and mission. As "artisan-missionary,"[29] Paul spent his tentmaking days in a workshop. According to Eckhard Schnabel, the workshop—along with the synagogue,[30] marketplace,[31] lecture hall,[32] and private house[33]—was one of the locations for Paul's missionary work in the city.[34] As Paul did his tentmaking tasks, he could have employed the workshop as an urban venue for preaching. His use of the workshop could have allowed him to proclaim and teach in a natural environment where he would have been able to meet people from all walks of life.[35] Though Paul engaged people in other social venues,[36] the workshop would have been a viable social setting to carry out

---

29. Hock, *Social Context*, 26.

30. During his missionary journeys, Paul went to synagogues in Salamis (Acts 13:5), Pisidian Antioch (13:14), Iconium (14:1), Thessalonica (17:1), Berea (17:10), Athens (17:17), Corinth (18:4), and Ephesus (18:19, 19:8). Even after his conversion, Paul preached in synagogues in Damascus (Acts 9:20).

31. Paul is explicitly mentioned as going to the marketplace (*agora*) "every day with those who happened to be there" (Acts 17:17).

32. Paul had discussions daily for two years at the lecture hall of Tyrannus in Ephesus (Acts 19:9–10).

33. The house (*oikos*) was an important missionary setting for Paul, especially the houses of Lydia in Philippi (Acts 16:15, 40), of the Philippian jailer (16:34), of Titius Justus in Corinth (18:7), of the unnamed owner in Troas (20:7–11), and of several believers in Ephesus (20:20). The houses that were cited with no explicit missionary task need to be included: Jason's house in Thessalonica (17:5–6), Aquila and Priscilla's house in Corinth (18:3), Philip's house in Caesarea (21:8), Mnason's house (21:16–17), and the houses of unidentified Christians in Tyre (21:3–5) and Ptolemais (21:7). House churches were also places of mission, like those in Antioch (Acts 11:26; 13:1, 30), Lystra, Iconium, and Pisidian Antioch (Acts 14:21–23).

34. Schnabel, *Paul the Missionary*, 288; cf. Haenchen, *Acts*, 512.

35. Meeks, *First Urban Christians*, 29.

36. The other social settings that Paul used for his mission are as follows: the residence of the proconsul of Cyprus, Sergius Paulus (Acts 13:6–12); the city gate in Lystra

his apostolic commission—realizing that Cynic philosophers were known to frequent workshops and enter into intellectual discourses there.[37] Hock posits the role of the workshop this way:

> To repeat: if the workshop was one social setting for Paul's missionary activity, it was also one of many. Indeed, the very variety of setting argues in favor of Paul having used the workshop to carry out his apostolic commission. Moreover, the regularity of Paul's presence in the workshop would argue that this social setting was as important a place for preaching as the synagogue and house, especially the latter since the synagogue, though obviously an oft-used setting, was hardly a permanent one.[38]

Schnabel speculates that Paul's tentmaking tasks in the workshop of Aquila and Priscilla (Acts 18:3) "would have brought Paul in contact with people who already trusted this couple—presumably not only Jews but also gentile customers."[39] These customers would have been persons whose occupations entailed much travel,[40] or persons who could travel in style.[41] Or they could have been people who had economic or financial objectives in coming to Paul: to buy, sell, deliver, or fetch goods. They could have been of different social standings: business owners or professionals, or slaves who were sent there on errands. Francois Tolmie comments that Paul's daily task as a tentmaker would have brought him into contact with people whom he would not have met in any other missionary setting.[42] From Paul's apostolic perspective, meeting such a wide variety of people in a workshop would be a benefit, because he would have been compelled to strike up informal conversations with customers and share the good news of God without regard to their social standing (Gal 3:26–28).

When Paul was in a city where he spent an extended period of time—like Corinth (Acts 18:1–18), Ephesus (Acts 19:1–20), or Thessalonica (1 Thess 2:6b–9)—he may have regularly practiced his trade. Ben

---

(14:7, 15–18); and the praetorium in Caesarea (24:24–26, 25:23–27).

37. Witherington, *Paul Quest*, 129. For more details on Cynic philosophers in workshops, see Hock, *Workshop as Social Setting*, 444–48.

38. Hock, "Workshop as Social Setting," 444.

39. Schnabel, *Paul the Missionary*, 298.

40. Murphy-O'Connor, *Paul's Corinth*, 192–93.

41. Hock, *Social Context*, 34. In this category, Onongha also includes the wealthy customers who used tents for covering during celebrations (Onongha, "Tentmaking," 186).

42. Tolmie, "Mission and the Workplace," 97; cf. Kistemaker, *Acts*, 650.

Witherington cites the possibility that in Corinth, the city where the Isthmian Games were held, many tourists would have come for the games and would have looked for a tent to rent or purchase.[43] This could have provided Paul with the opportune time to reach all sorts of people.

Thus, in cities that required Paul to stay for a considerable time and during occasions when he saw an opportunity or need, Paul would have used his tentmaking skills at a workshop, where he would have had appropriate engagements with people of different walks of life, to talk with them about Jesus and the hope that he brings. Just as Paul availed himself of opportunities for mission activity in synagogues, houses, lecture halls, and marketplaces, he could have used the workshop as a place for gospel conversations or topics on the kingdom of God.

Paul's Willingness to Suffer as Tentmaker

So far, we have covered the first two descriptions of Paul's experience as a tentmaker—shared and team labor and ministry and use of the workshop as a social venue for connection and mission. The third description is his willingness to suffer as a tentmaker and missionary. Paul frequently described his ministry in terms of toil and labor.[44] He even used the language of manual toil or physical labor in juxtaposition with his apostolic work and perils. In the first of the five hardship, or affliction (*peristasis*), catalogues[45] in the Corinthian correspondence (1 Cor 4:11–12), we see the list of sufferings that Paul underwent when he toiled as a tentmaker and ministered as an apostle.[46] In this first list, Paul spoke of his being hungry, thirsty, poorly clothed, beaten, and homeless "to the present hour" (1 Cor 4:11a) as being closely linked to the work of his hands. Similarly, the third catalogue of afflictions also mentions Paul's experience of hunger, thirst, shortage of food, and lack of clothing (2 Cor 11:27)—hardships that were put side by side with his difficulties and dangers in ministry (2 Cor 11:23–26, 28). In other words, Paul placed "his exhausting toil alongside other apostolic perils."[47]

43. Witherington, *Paul Quest*, 128; cf. Capes et al., *Rediscovering Paul*, 103.

44. Meggitt, *Paul, Poverty, and Survival*, 89. For instances in Paul's letters, see Rom 16:6, 12; 1 Cor 3:13–15; 15:10, 58; 16:16; Phil 1:6, 30; 1 Thess 1:3; 5:12, 17.

45. Fredrickson, "Paul, Hardships, and Suffering," 172–97; cf. Fitzgerald, *Cracks*.

46. The other four lists are found in 2 Cor 4:7–12, 6:4–5, 11:23–29, and 12:10. Cf. Rom 8:35–36.

47. Still, "Did Paul Loathe," 787.

In addition, Paul reminded the Thessalonian believers that he and his missionary team (i.e., Timothy and Silas) worked night and day "while we proclaimed to you the gospel of God" (1 Thess 2:9a). The purpose of such toil and labor as tentmakers while they did their mission was for them not to be a burden to the Thessalonians (2 Thess 2:9b). Paul echoed this statement in his second letter to them: "But with toil and labor we worked night and day, so that we might not burden any of you" (2 Thess 3:8b). Regarding this repeated statement, Abraham Malherbe points out that Paul "thus wishes to convey, not just that he worked, but the strenuous and exhausting demand of labor on him, which he had undertaken willingly out of his love for them."[48] Whether he served as a tentmaker or missionary, Paul did his toil and labor out of love for people. Margaret Thrall rightly comments that Paul "engaged in manual labour, not to accumulate wealth and thus to achieve status elevation, but to keep himself in economic necessities whilst he pursued his main tasks of evangelism and pastoral nurture."[49]

Paul's suffering was not only due to the difficulties and perils of work and ministry, it was also because of the lowly status and stigma associated with being an artisan (including a tentmaker). The Greco-Roman elite considered working with one's hands demeaning.[50] Hock pictured artisans as stigmatized workers who were slavish, considered unnecessary, and frequently reviled, abused, or victimized (though not as lowly as unskilled workers or miners).[51] In light of the stigmatized status of artisans, Hock describes Paul's situation this way:

> Traveling and plying a trade were always exhausting and were frequently painful; consequently, he could always summarize his experiences in catalogues of sufferings.... Paul's travels, like those of other itinerant artisans and teachers, were often punctuated by delays, difficulties, and dangers.... Making tents meant rising before dawn, toiling until sunset with leather, knives, and awls, and accepting the various social stigmas and humiliations that were part of the artisan's lot, not to mention the poverty—being cold, hungry, and poorly clothed.[52]

48. Malherbe, *Thessalonians*, 148.

49. Thrall, *Corinthians*, 2:704.

50. Witherington, *Paul Quest*, 82. However, Witherington noted that first-century Jews and Greco-Roman artisans did not share this view. Cf. MacMullen, *Roman Social Relations*, 7383.

51. Hock, *Social Context*, 36.

52. Hock, *Social Context*, 37.

However, despite all his difficulties as a tentmaker and perils as an apostle, Paul was not disillusioned. Paul could still confidently describe his experience this way: "Sorrowful, yet always rejoicing; as poor, yet making many rich; as having nothing, and yet possessing everything" (2 Cor 6:10). In relation to Paul's work situation, Timothy Savage observes that although Paul could write about his labor in harsh terms, "he always stops short of disparaging work itself.... (He) follows a line of Jewish tradition by maintaining that while work can be exhausting it is never demeaning."[53] Though Paul clearly described his toil and labor as including difficulty and suffering, he did not hold a negative view of his tentmaking trade.[54]

Reflections on Paul's Experience as Tentmaker

In conclusion, let us now briefly reflect on Paul's tentmaking experience. Paul had a clear self-identity not only as an apostle but also as a tentmaker, realizing that both were closely tied to his giftedness and what God had called him to be and do. Such double self-understanding gave him a keen sense of vocation from God. Wherever, whenever, and from whoever Paul may have learned his trade, what is important is that he learned to use his gifts (including his skills related to tentmaking) to serve God and others.

In addition, knowing why Paul engaged in tentmaking can help us understand a glimpse of Paul's satisfaction, meaning, and purpose as a tentmaker, even though it entailed difficulty and suffering. Having learned of Paul's use of his trade as an integral part of God's apostolic mission for him makes us appreciate his holistic approach to life and ministry—making us grasp that employing the workshop as a social venue was a natural and viable way to meet and engage different kinds of people with various social standings. These were individuals whom he would not have met if he did not practice his trade.

We also see the value of Paul's experience of involving partners in accomplishing the mission of God for him. In his three missionary journeys, he never traveled alone. When he traveled with his team, he toiled and ministered with them—sharing the load of missionary work and manual

---

53. Savage, *Power through Weakness*, 86.

54. See Still, "Did Paul Loathe." For an alternative view (that Paul viewed his work negatively), see Hock's contentions in *Social Context*, 66–67; "Paul's Tentmaking," 560–62. Hock argues that Paul's view of his trade and work was negative.

labor. Paul understood that holistic ministry was to be implemented in community and in the whole of life.

In relation to tentmaking in the current Canadian or Western society, Paul's experience can help us, as twenty-first-century tentmakers,[55] to perceive the benefits of affirming the value of core satisfiers in multivocational ministry (like having clarity in one's identity that is linked to a holistic approach to life, relationships, and service). Paul's experience can also aid us in welcoming the reality of stressors in everyday tentmaking (that toil and labor include difficulties and sufferings). What can remind us not to be overwhelmed by stressors and to be cognizant of the joy of satisfiers is knowing (as well as remembering) why we are engaged in both pastoral and marketplace mission—just as Paul knew that his trade enabled him to not become a burden to anyone and that tentmaking took away any hindrance to the gospel.

Since multivocational ministers need to be engaged in the whole of life, we also need to develop relationships of trust (like Paul did with his missionary teams), to discover and use our gifts with others (just as Paul and his teams engaged in toil and labor). Finally, we need to share the load of ministry with partners from different walks of life in order to become all things to all people and by all means save some.

Questions for Reflection

1. In your own understanding, why do you think tentmaking was important to Paul and his mission from God?
2. What do you think motivated Paul to continue in his labor and toil as a tentmaker and missionary, despite the hardship and suffering that both tentmaking and mission work entail?
3. In your own tentmaking or ministry, what insight or lesson from Paul's tentmaking experience resonates most to you? Why does it resonate the most?

---

55. I am also a multivocational minister, serving full-time in a seminary faculty and part-time as a pastor in two churches that I took part in planting when our church in the Philippines sent my family and me as missionaries to Canada in 2007. Each of these two churches now has three tentmaking pastors who minister as a pastoral team and according to our gift mix.

Bibliography

Agrell, Göran. *Work, Toil, and Sustenance: An Examination of the View of Work in the New Testament, Taking into Consideration Views Found in Old Testament, Intertestamental, and Early Rabbinic Writings*. Stockholm: Verbum, 1976.

Barclay, William. *The Acts of the Apostles*. Philadelphia: Westminster, 1976.

Barnett, P. W. "Tentmaking." In *Dictionary of Paul and His Letters*, edited by Gerald F. Hawthorne et al., 925–27. Downers Grove, IL: InterVarsity, 1993.

Bornkamm, Günther. *Paul*. Translated by D. M. G. Stalker. Philadelphia: Fortress, 1995.

Bruce, F. F. *Paul: Apostle of the Heart Set Free*. Grand Rapids: Eerdmans, 1977.

Capes, David B., et al. *Rediscovering Paul: An Introduction to His World, Letters, and Theology*. Downers Grove, IL: InterVarsity, 2007.

Deismann, Adolf. *Paul: A Study in Social and Religious History*. New York: Hodder & Stoughton, 1926.

Dunn, James D. G. *The Theology of Paul the Apostle*. Grand Rapids: Eerdmans, 1998.

Elwell, Walter A., ed. *Baker Encyclopedia of the Bible*. Grand Rapids: Baker, 1988.

Fitzgerald, John T. *Cracks in an Earthen Vessel: An Examination of the Catalogues of Hardships in the Corinthian Correspondence*. Society of Biblical Literature Dissertation Series 99. Atlanta: Scholars, 1988.

Fredrickson, David E. "Paul, Hardships, and Suffering." In *Paul in the Greco-Roman World: A Handbook*, edited by J. Paul Sampley, 172–97. Harrisburg, PA: Trinity, 2003.

Haenchen, Ernst. *The Acts of the Apostles: A Commentary*. Philadelphia: Westminster, 1971.

Heyer, C. J. den. *Paul: A Man of Two Worlds*. Translated by John Bowden. Harrisburg, PA: Trinity, 2000.

Hock, Ronald F. "Paul's Tentmaking and the Problem of His Social Class." *Journal of Biblical Literature* 97.4 (1978) 555–64. https://doi.org/10.2307/3265397.

———. *The Social Context of Paul's Ministry: Tentmaking and Apostleship*. Philadelphia: Fortress, 1980.

———. "Workshop as Social Setting for Paul's Missionary Preaching." *Catholic Biblical Quarterly* 41 (1979) 438–50.

Horrell, David G. *The Social Ethos of the Corinthian Correspondence: Interests and Ideology from 1 Corinthians to 1 Clement*. Studies of the New Testament and its World. Edinburgh: T. & T. Clark, 1996.

Kistemaker, Simon J. *Exposition of the Acts of the Apostles*. Grand Rapids: Baker, 1990.

Kritzinger, J. J. *'N Missionêre bediening: op weg na strukture vir'n jong kerk*. Pretoria: N. G. Kerkboekhandel, 1979.

Longnecker, Richard N. *Acts*. In *The Expositor's Bible Commentary*, edited by Tremper Longman III and David E. Garland. Rev. ed. Grand Rapids: Zondervan, 2017.

MacMullen, Ramsey. *Roman Social Relations 50 B.C. to A.D. 284*. New Haven, CT: Yale University Press, 1974.

Malherbe, Abraham J. *The Letters to the Thessalonians: A New Translation with Introduction and Commentary*. The Anchor Bible 32B. New Haven, CT: Yale University Press, 2008.

Marshall, Peter. *Enmity in Corinth: Social Conventions in Paul's Relations with the Corinthians*. Tübingen, Germany: JCB Mohr, 1987.

Meeks, Wayne A. *The First Urban Christians: The Social World of the Apostle Paul*. New Haven, CT: Yale University Press, 1983.

Meggitt, Justin J. *Paul, Poverty and Survival. Studies of the New Testament and its World.* Edinburgh: T. & T. Clark, 1998.

Michaelis, W. "*Skenopoios*." *TDNT* (1971) 393–94.

Murphy-O'Connor, Jerome. *Paul: A Critical Life.* Oxford: Oxford University Press, 1996.

———. *St. Paul's Corinth: Texts and Archaeology.* Collegeville, MN: Liturgical, 2002.

Onongha, Kelvin. "Tentmaking in the Twenty-First Century: Theological and Missiological Implications for Contemporary Adventist Missions." *Andrews Univeristy Seminary Studies* 53 (2015) 183–96.

Picirilli, Robert E. *Paul the Apostle.* Chicago: Moody, 1986.

Polhill, John. *Paul and His Letters.* Nashville: Broadman & Holman, 1999.

Reisner, Rainer. *Paul's Early Period: Chronology, Mission Strategy, Theology.* Translated by Doug Stott. Grand Rapids: Eerdmans, 1998.

Robbins, Vernon K. *The Tapestry of Early Christian Discourse: Rhetoric, Society, and Ideology.* New York: Routledge, 1996.

Savage, Timothy B. *Power through Weakness: Paul's Understanding of the Christian Ministry in Corinthians.* Cambridge: Cambridge University Press, 1995.

Schnabel, Eckhard J. *Paul the Missionary: Realities, Strategies, and Methods.* Downers Grove, IL: IVP Academic, 2008.

Schnelle, Udo. *Apostle Paul: His Life and Theology.* Ada, MI: Baker, 2012.

Smith, Abraham. "Tentmaker." In *The New Interpreter's Dictionary of the Bible*, edited by Katharine D. Sakenfield, 523. Nashville: Abingdon, 2009.

Still, Todd D. "Did Paul Loathe Manual Labor? Revisiting the Work of Ronald F. Hock on the Apostle's Tentmaking and Social Class." *Journal of Biblical Literature* 125.4 (2006) 781–95. https://doi.org/10.2307/27638405.

Thompson, John A. "Trades and Occupations." In *Baker Encyclopedia of the Bible*, edited by Walter A. Elwell, 2083–93. Grand Rapids: Baker, 1988.

Thrall, Margaret E. *A Critical and Exegetical Commentary on the Second Epistle to the Corinthians.* 2 vols. London: T. & T. Clark, 2000.

Throckmorton, B. H. "Tentmaker." In *The Interpreter's Dictionary of the Bible*, edited by George A. Buttrick, 537. Nashville: Abingdon, 1962.

Tolmie, Francois. "Mission and the Workplace—the Example of Paul." *Journal for Christian Scholarship* 53 (2017) 91–105.

Wessels, Johannes Mattheus. "Contextual Views on Paul the Tentmaker." *Missionalia* 46 (2018) 5–23.

Witherington, Ben III. *The Paul Quest: The Renewed Search for the Jew of Tarsus.* Westmont, IL: IVP Academic, 2001.

Wolff, Christian. "Humility and Self-Denial in Jesus' Life and Message and in the Apostolic Existence of Paul." In *Paul and Jesus: Collected Essays*, edited by Alexander J. M. Wedderburn, 145–60. Sheffield, UK: Sheffield Academic Press, 1989.

4

Charism, Vocation, and Work: Theological Reflections on Tentmaking

James E. Pedlar

> I was but a novice, a young, raw disciple, unskilled in the word of righteousness; but faith in Christ, and the love of God in my heart, overcame all the powers of darkness. I found unspeakable pleasure in doing and suffering the will of God. I laboured diligently with my hands; I owed no man anything; I had enough for myself, and a little to spare for others; I attended four or five meetings every week; we prayed, sang hymns, read the Bible, and exhorted one another to fear and love God. The power of the Lord was present to heal; He owned His own work, and gave us prosperity.[1]

SO WROTE CHRISTOPHER HOPPER of his early forays into ministry in 1743. He was a farmer's son born in Ryton, County Durham, in 1722, and worked transporting coal by wagon for a few years before he was converted in the early years of the Methodist revival. At this stage, Methodist ministry structures were still evolving and somewhat fluid. Though Hopper was not designated as a "preacher," he was clearly leading worship and "exhorting" fellow believers in ways that most Christians would find indistinguishable from preaching. Though he was working full-time, his ministry extended

---

1. Jackson, *Early Methodist Preachers*, 190.

beyond his local community, making him somewhat of a traveling preacher from soon after his conversion.[2]

Hopper's preaching was simply a natural expression of his newfound faith and his concern for the salvation of his neighbors, and so he began preaching without much thought. He wrote, "As yet, I had not examined my call to preach the Gospel, nor considered the consequences of such an undertaking."[3] But the harsh opposition that he and other Methodist lay preachers faced soon forced him to deeper reflection, out of which he concluded that his call to preach was "consistent with Scripture, reason, and experience."[4] Hopper continued "tentmaking" as a schoolteacher for several years.

> My time was employed six days in teaching the children under my care the branches of learning I professed, and the first principles of Christianity. I spent every Sabbath, and all my vacant hours, in preaching, reading, praying, visiting the sick, and conversing with all that Providence put in my way. God was with me and blessed my weak labours.[5]

Eventually, in 1749, Hopper gave up his paid employment, though he could see no prospects beyond "beggary and great afflictions," because, as he wrote, "the work of God so increased in my hands, that I could not properly attend it."[6] He was soon formally recognized as an itinerant preacher in John Wesley's Methodist movement and would continue in this role for forty-seven years.[7]

Hopper is just one of a vast army of lay preachers who gave leadership to early Methodism. Without enough support from ordained leaders in the Church of England, John Wesley felt he had no other choice than to use laypersons to provide preaching and pastoral guidance to his Methodist societies. Over time, some of these preachers would be classed as "local

---

2. So he writes, "I had one invitation after another, to High-Spenn [now High Spen], Barlow, Woodside, Predhoe, Newlands, Blanchland, Durham, Sunderland, and many other places" (Jackson, *Early Methodist Preachers*, 190). Though his ministry was mainly among the Methodists, he preached outdoors to all sorts of people and mentioned preaching among the Quakers several times in 1747 (Jackson, *Early Methodist Preachers*, 197).

3. Jackson, *Early Methodist Preachers*, 191.

4. Jackson, *Early Methodist Preachers*, 194.

5. Jackson, *Early Methodist Preachers*, 195.

6. Jackson, *Early Methodist Preachers*, 199.

7. Vickers, *Dictionary of Methodism*.

preachers," while others were "traveling preachers," or itinerants. Itinerants were given financial support so that they did not have to work, while local preachers had other jobs to support themselves and their families. A typical path to itinerant ministry was to begin as a local preacher, as did Hopper. In the following century, local preachers would continue to serve as laypeople, while the itinerancy developed into an ordained, pastoral office.[8] However, in the earliest days of Methodism, John Wesley did not see itinerants as different from local preachers. Rather, they were "one species, who differed only in the extent and location of their work."[9] Although Hopper remained a traveling preacher and never returned to other paid employment, there were examples of itinerants who returned to work as local preachers, and even "half-itinerants."[10]

I begin with Hopper because he highlights an important historical reality: church leadership has come in a variety of forms, paid and unpaid. Western Christians in the early twenty-first century tend to think of full-time paid ministry as the norm, but this has not always been the case. Christopher Hopper began fulfilling a pastoral function as a preacher and shepherd long before it was his full-time employment, and there was no fundamental difference between his "part-time" ministry as a local preacher and his later full-time itinerant ministry. He was doing the same ministry, using the same gifts, and fulfilling the same vocation.

The recognition of tentmaking ministry in Western contexts presses us to examine our theology of ministry and relate it to the theology of work. A deeper reflection on tentmaking helps us to see that all Christians are multivocational, and that tentmaking is not a compromise of pastoral vocation but simply a different configuration of the pastor's vocational responsibilities.

Charism and Vocation

The theology of ministry begins with the charisms of the Spirit, or spiritual gifts. "Charism" is a transliteration of *charisma*, a term possibly coined by the apostle Paul.[11] It is a variant of *charis*, and its basic meaning is "the con-

---

8. See Bowmer, *Pastor and People*, 198–228.
9. Batty, "Origins," 20.
10. Batty, "Origins," 20–21.
11. The following section is a condensation of my exposition of the theology of charisms in *Division, Diversity, and Unity*, 15–21. On the origins of the term, see Dunn, *Jesus and the Spirit*, 205–6.

crete result of the bestowal" of grace.¹² This has to be distinguished from the popular understanding of "charisma," which is heavily influenced by sociologist Max Weber's concept of charismatic authority.¹³ On the other hand, it must also be distinguished from colloquial Christian understandings of "charismatic" as a type of spirituality that emphasizes spectacular manifestations of the Spirit. This is closer to the biblical concept, but the focus on conspicuously miraculous gifts is not justified scripturally. Paul focuses on the gifts of prophecy and tongues in 1 Cor 12–14, but he also includes seemingly mundane activities such as teaching, pastoring, administration, helping, and giving in his lists of charisms (1 Cor 12:28–30, Rom 12:6–8, Eph 4:11). If we strip away the common understandings of the term, then, how might we articulate a more biblical theology of charisms?

First, while the Greek term *charisma* sometimes refers to any bestowal of grace (e.g., 2 Cor 1:11) or the gift of salvation (Rom 5:15–16, 6:23), in the New Testament, charisms normally refer to diverse personal gifts of grace. These personal charisms differ "according to the grace given to us" (Rom 12:6) and are distributed as the Spirit chooses (1 Cor 12:11). Second, charisms are not necessarily "spectacular" manifestations of the Spirit, as noted above. Those of us who are spiritual, Paul says, recognize that everything we have has been received from God's hand (1 Cor 3:21–23, 4:7), and the gifts he gives may build upon and elevate the "natural" abilities he has given us. Third, charisms are vocational gifts. They are not given for the benefit of the recipient but for the "common good" (1 Cor 12:7). Charism and vocation are not the same thing, but they are inextricably linked; hence the parallelism between "gifts" (*charismata*), "services" (*diakonia*), and "activities" (*energemata*) in 1 Cor 12:4–6. A charism is a gift of grace that enables and obliges the recipient to take up a vocation, and a Christian vocation presupposes its corresponding charism. Fourth, charisms are not necessarily sanctifying gifts.¹⁴ Normally, Christians exercising their charism grow in holiness; however, the case of the Corinthian church demonstrates that charisms are also given to the spiritually immature, and they may create division and strife. Paul does not cast doubt on the charisms of the Corinthians, though he calls them to a more faithful and mature exercise

---

12. Njiru, *Holy Spirit's Activity*, 76.

13. Weber, *Max Weber on Charisma*, 19–20.

14. Thomas Aquinas made a strong distinction between charisms (*gratiae gratis datae*) and sanctifying grace (*gratia gratum faciens*). Charisms are ordered to the sanctification of others (Aquinas, *Gospel of Grace*, 125–44 (Q. 111); Aquinas, *Prophecy*).

of their gifts. Fifth, charisms are not self-authenticating; they are subject to discernment, evaluation, and oversight. Paul sets out a test for charisms in 1 Cor 12:3—their bearers must acknowledge the lordship of Christ. This is because, from a Christian perspective, divine grace is Christ centered in its source and its goal. Charisms, therefore, are not simply "gifts" in any sense but varied personal manifestations of the great gift of salvation in Christ, wrought by the Spirit. Charisms can also be evaluated by their fruitfulness in building up the church, as Paul suggests in 1 Cor 14:26. In either case, the charismatic individual is subject to the judgment of the community. Local pastors exercise such oversight in their congregations, helping God's people to discern their charisms and helping to coordinate the fruitful integration of charisms on a local level. Pastors are inevitably subject to oversight of their own, though this varies widely depending on church polity, and such oversight itself must be seen as a charismatically enabled vocation.[15] Sixth, charisms have an interdependent character. This is the obvious implication of the analogy of the body and its parts in 1 Cor 12: each member is organically dependent upon the whole. Seventh, charisms have a provisional character in relation to the eschaton and are subordinate to the enduring divine gift of love. The so-called "love chapter" (1 Cor 13), oft used at wedding ceremonies in isolation, is in fact the centerpiece in Paul's treatment of charisms in 1 Cor 12–14.[16] The charisms will fade and cease, but love will never end.

Imago Dei, Vocation, and Work

So, charisms are diverse gifts of grace given to persons in the church that bring a vocational obligation. But a fuller view of Christian vocation must begin with the creation of humanity in the image of God and the accompanying commission given to humanity: "Be fruitful and increase in number; fill the earth and subdue it. Rule over the fish of the sea and the birds of the air and over every living creature that moves on the ground" (Gen 1:28 NIV). All human creatures were given a vocation to "rule" or exercise "dominion," but such terms are easily misunderstood if they are not interpreted with reference to the God who confers this commission. Human dominion is not a license for domination or exploitation, since it is meant to "image"

---

15. See the discussion of oversight as charism with reference to recent ecumenical dialogue in Pedlar, *Division, Diversity, and Unity*, 67–68.
16. Njiru, *Holy Spirit's Activity*, 31–68.

God's loving and just rule. Moreover, human rule of creation is delegated and therefore subject to divine accountability. For this reason, though the word is not in the text, one could say that humans have a vocation to be stewards of creation. Further, in Gen 2, Adam was tasked with working and taking care of the garden of Eden (Gen 2:15). Here, we see a call to cultivate the land, as well as the task of naming the animals (Gen 2:19–20), which implies management of the animal world (cf. Ps 8:6–8).

Thus, the image of God provides the basis for an ethic of creation stewardship or creation care, but there are much broader implications for this call to the cultivation of the land. As Richard Middleton so helpfully points out in his book *A New Heaven and a New Earth*, agriculture is in fact the basis of all culture. Without agriculture, human civilization could not develop beyond the sophistication of a hunter–gatherer society. Agriculture is necessary to the building of cities and towns and the diversification of an economy. The human vocation to exercise dominion over creation and cultivate the land, therefore, can be seen in its broadest application as a cultural mandate, or calling to build civilization in a way that glorifies God and fosters human flourishing.[17] Every one of us has a part to play in this collective calling. The functioning of human society requires a vast array of domestic, community, and economic activity in which all people participate. Therefore, our participation in "secular" society is not foreign to Christian vocation. Every way that my daily life contributes to human flourishing is a part of my sacred calling. I am called to be a son, father, husband, brother, uncle, neighbor, taxpayer, voter, seminary professor, etc., and in each of these vocations I am tasked with glorifying God and contributing to human flourishing. This is the basis for a theology of work which breaks down traditional barriers between "sacred" and "secular." The work of a teacher, barber, or farm laborer is dignified and sacralized by virtue of its contribution to human civilization, in fulfillment of the calling given to humanity as God's image bearers. In our various family and community roles, as well as the ministries we take on in the church, we are fulfilling God's calling for our lives.

Tentmaking and Multivocational Ministry

This broader view of vocation, including both the cultural mandate and our charismatic vocations, changes the conversation about tentmaking.

17. Middleton, *New Heaven*, 41–43.

All Christians are multivocational. All of us fulfill various vocations, some of which foster human flourishing in a broader sense and some of which build up the church according to our charisms. Both tentmakers and full-time pastors have vocational obligations to friends, family members, and their communities. Sometimes these various vocations come into conflict and must be carefully balanced. That is why Paul recognized that single persons have greater freedom for ministry than those who are married (1 Cor 7:32–34). Yet, even single persons are embedded in other familial and community relationships that make vocational demands upon them.

If we are all multivocational, what distinguishes tentmaking from other types of pastoral ministry? It is not that tentmakers have less time to fulfill their vocation, since their other paid work is still part of their contribution to human flourishing and therefore is part of their sacred calling. Rather, tentmaking pastors are simply serving in the vocational economy with a different configuration of responsibilities. They are giving more of their time to the common good and less to the good of the church. But tentmakers must resist the temptation to see their non-church paid work as unholy or undignified. No doubt the tentmaking pastor will face challenges that a person in full-time pastoral ministry will not face, somewhat akin to the way a married pastor has burdens on their time that a single person does not have. The pressures on tentmakers, however, are partly due to cultural expectations of pastors in contexts where full-time pastoring is assumed as the norm and pastors are often expected to carry an unhealthy portion of the ministry of the whole congregation. A tentmaking ministry arrangement may free the local church from some of the bad habits of "clericalization" if the congregation recognizes the opportunity and endeavors to release its members more fully into ministry.

That was certainly the experience of the early Methodists. The shortage of ordained leadership forced the Methodist movement to raise up a vast array of lay leaders like Christopher Hopper. They experimented with different models of paid and unpaid pastoral leadership by necessity, but the benefit was that many people were empowered to exercise their charisms and further the work of God. Their seemingly irregular forms of ministry brought ridicule from critics, but they provided a nimble structure that enabled the movement to rapidly expand with little resources.

The way that pastors are compensated is not fundamental to our theology of ministry. What is fundamental are the charism and vocation that is given by the Spirit according to divine providence and our common vocation to contribute to human flourishing. All of us must find ways to live out our various vocations in all their fullness, and a mixture of pastoral ministry with other paid work is not a compromise of the pastoral vocation. This truth should embolden us to move forward in faith, believing that God will continue to supply all our needs in Christ, even as we grapple with forms of ministry that seem unfamiliar to us. It may be that tentmaking fosters the kind of responsive and flexible leadership needed for renewal in our time.

Questions for Reflection

1. What would you identify as your charisms? What roles do you serve with them?
2. How do you relate the *imago Dei*, vocation, and work to each other? What does this mean for how you view your work responsibilities?
3. If "we are all multivocational," how does that impact your life?

Bibliography

Aquinas, Thomas. *The Gospel of Grace (1a2æ. 106–114)*. Vol. 30 of *Summa Theologiae*. Translated by Cornelius Ernst. Cambridge: Cambridge University Press, 2006.
———. *Prophecy and Other Charisms (2a2æ. 171–8)*. Vol. 45 of *Summa Theologiae*. Translated by Roland Potter. Cambridge: Cambridge University Press, 2006.
Batty, Margaret. "Origins: The Age of Wesley." In *Workaday Preachers: The Story of Methodist Local Preaching*, edited by Geoffery Milburn and Margaret Batty, 11–34. Peterborough, UK: Methodist Publishing House, 1995.
Bowmer, John C. *Pastor and People: A Study of Church and Ministry in Wesleyan Methodism from the Death of John Wesley (1791) to the Death of Jabez Bunting (1858)*. London: Epworth, 1975.
Dunn, James D. G. *Jesus and the Spirit: A Study of the Religious and Charismatic Experience of Jesus and the First Christians as Reflected in the New Testament*. London: SCM, 1975.
Jackson, Thomas, ed. *The Lives of Early Methodist Preachers*. 4th ed. Vol. 1. London: Wesleyan Conference Office, 1875.
Middleton, J. Richard. *A New Heaven and a New Earth: Reclaiming Biblical Eschatology*. Grand Rapids: Baker Academic, 2014.
Njiru, Paul Kariuki. *Charisms and the Holy Spirit's Activity in the Body of Christ: An Exegetical-Theological Study of 1 Corinthians 12:4–11 and Romans 12:6–8*. Rome: Pontificia Università Gregoriana, 2002.

Pedlar, James E. *Division, Diversity, and Unity: A Theology of Ecclesial Charisms.* New York: Peter Lang, 2015.

Vickers, John A. *Dictionary of Methodism in Britain and Ireland.* UK: Wesley Historical Society, 2008. https://dmbi.online/.

Weber, Max. *Max Weber on Charisma and Institution Building.* Edited by S. L. Eisenstadt. Chicago: University of Chicago Press, 1968.

Part 3

Issues Arising from Multivocational Ministry

5

The Tentmaking Home as Sanctuary

MARILYN DRAPER AND MARK D. CHAPMAN

DISCUSSIONS ON TENTMAKING IN the Canadian context focus on the interweaving of Christian ministry and employment.[1] However, tentmakers may find themselves unprepared for the stresses that erupt in their personal lives if they neglect to examine their assumptions regarding how tentmaking ministry interacts with their homelife.

Rather than offering a set of step-by-step instructions on how to reorganize their homes or better use their time, this chapter offers a practical theology by suggesting three ways that tentmakers might reframe their homes as a sanctuary. It should be understood that "Practical Theology is critical, theological reflection on the practices of the Church as they interact with the practices of the world, with a view to ensuring and enabling faithful participation in God's redemptive practices in, to and for the world."[2] First, the home can be a place of refuge. Second, the home can be a place of hospitality. Third, and most important, the home can be a place of worship. These three images provide hope by reframing the home through the lens of an integrated incarnational ministry where tentmakers and their families can experience more fully the presence of God infusing their daily life as they participate in Christ's mission in the world. As David Fitch claims, "Faithful presence is cooperating with God where he

---

1. See Watson and Santos, "Tentmaking."
2. Swinton, *Practical Theology*, 6.

is already present."[3] As a foundation for this discussion, we begin with an examination of the experiences of tentmakers at home to explain why this theological reframing is necessary.

Challenges for Tentmakers at Home

Tentmaking ministry is often added on to an already busy employment schedule, or employment is added to a full ministry schedule. Thus, the tentmaker has little opportunity to intentionally consider how the homelife will be affected by potentially conflicting responsibilities. It is therefore not surprising that many tentmakers in the Canadian Multivocational Ministry Project (CMMP) spoke of challenges they faced at home.

Canadian Multivocational Leaders and the Home

While tentmakers' navigation of homelife was not a specific focus of the CMMP, interviewees provided glimpses into the challenges faced by tentmakers and their families, specifically concerning their use of time and need for boundaries in their homelife. In *The Art and Practice of Bivocational Ministry*, Dennis Bickers states that "time is the number one challenge" of tentmakers.[4] Couples struggled to find time together or quality time for family. "It's really difficult not to have ministry be a 24/7 event," explained one couple. Yet, participants sought ways to connect with one another at home:

> Gosh I think that's why, one of the reasons why my wife and I stay up late because we try to find time, you know, just prior to the kids going to bed . . . we look for opportunities to connect . . . we knew this hectic life was going to take place so we made a conscious decision . . . to meet each other in prayer every morning.

Tentmakers wrestle with schedules and boundaries, particularly when work, ministry, and family are all in the same physical area of the home. Some project participants developed detailed schedules: "You know you need to have systems in place on a weekly calendar to guard your family time . . . especially for your marriage." Others set priorities: "I've been working really hard to make sure that I have family time set aside, that my

---

3. Fitch, *Faithful Presence*, 184.
4. Bickers, *Bivocational Ministry*, 29.

job isn't my only priority." Some couples recognized their need for boundary setting: "So we're just very conscientious about . . . having boundaries on both space and time in order to make it clear to one another when and where things are happening." One tentmaker admitted to having "difficulty in my life keeping the church work and personal work separate." Tentmakers are juggling time, organization, and boundary setting in an attempt to balance home, work, and ministry. A glimpse into Marilyn's story illustrates how this might not be an issue of balance but of framing.

The Surprises of Tentmaking: Marilyn's Experience

When the decision was made to move to tentmaking ministry, my husband and I already had a busy household. We were running our restoration business full-time out of our home. Our four children were all under ten years of age. We were well connected with our neighborhood and had a constant stream of interactions with people in our community. We were recently ordained and actively involved in congregational ministry. Adding the development of a church plant was a ministry to which we felt called but one that brought additional costs rather than remuneration. Thus, the decision was made to continue running our business as we started the new congregation.

However, while both of us had the benefit of theological training and ministry experience, none of our preparation focused on adapting homelife. Our assessment as church planters examined our ability to lead, to start new initiatives, and to build relationships. Our theological training emphasized our understanding of the church and the essential nature of the gospel. Our examination of ministry initiatives focused on establishing goals and articulating vision and strategy. Only when we were into the thick of ministry, business, and life did we realize that we had virtually no boundaries. The merging of all three spheres centered around our family home. The excessive activity, people coming and going, and pressures on our time increased the sense of vulnerability and stress experienced by all family members. My husband found that the business, community needs, local ministerial leadership, children's activities, and church responsibilities all competed for his time and attention. In my efforts to be involved in our children's schools, navigate schedules, keep our home presentable, give pastoral support to congregants, and provide teaching for the church plant, I began to experience burnout.

PART 3 | ISSUES ARISING FROM MULTIVOCATIONAL MINISTRY

Fortunately, we survived our foray into tentmaking. In fact, through the years, we have been on the leadership teams of several church plants. My husband and I continue to enjoy opportunities to minister and work together. Our children benefitted from their experiences of meeting the variety of people who have shared a meal at our dinner table. We witnessed God's power to change lives.

Further, we have learned that much of ministry is simply noticing how God shows up in the activities of everyday life. I suspect that if we had developed a practical theology of our homelife earlier, we might have been able to predict the pressures and address the challenges with less angst and more clarity. By recognizing that we do ministry in the midst of our struggles instead of in spite of our struggles, we continue to find ways to cooperate even more fully and more freely with what the Spirit of God seeks to do in our midst. To do this, we had to theologically reframe our view of the home.

Theologically Reframing Our View of the Home as Sanctuary

Reframing how we see our homes through an incarnational-ministry lens may release tentmakers from guilt and self-accusation arising from a sense of inadequacy regarding use of time and boundary setting. Bickers writes, "Until bivocational ministers learn how to balance their priorities, they will struggle in every area of their lives, and their ministries will be less effective and less enjoyable than they could be."[5] When tentmakers hear this emphasis, they are tempted to think that they are responsible for their own frustrations. They can assume that employment and ministry concern productivity. When the focus is on productivity, then the home becomes solely the base from which the tentmaker performs the more important work of ministry. While learning to set priorities, manage our time, and seek intentional balance are helpful practical skills, perhaps it is our view of home that needs examination. In reframing, tentmakers are invited to see their homes as the foundational, integrated place of ministry, because in the home God's presence intersects with our humanity and leads us to worship.

Scripture is rich with imagery about home and God dwelling with his people where they live, from the garden of Eden onward.[6] Abraham and

---

5. Bickers, *Bivocational Ministry*, 113.
6. Fitch, *Faithful Presence*, 21–24.

Sarah discover home as the place of encounter with the divine (Gen 18). In the Old Testament, God's words permeate Israelite homes: "Teach them to your children, talking about them when you are at home . . . when you lie down and when you rise" (Deut 11:19). Even the Christian life is described as a home. Jesus said the triune God inhabits God's people: "we will come and make our home with them" (John 14:23).

Theological reframing invites God's active presence in the home. Fitch explains, "God has not left us. We, in all our striving and independence, have not allowed any space for him to be present between us and the people we do live with."[7] Fortunately, hope emerges when we start to acknowledge that God is present and active in our homelife: "When we sit face to face, listening and tending to what's going on in the other person, and when we do the same thing together with God, amazing transformation and goodness begins."[8] Incarnational ministry reminds us that God is with us in the midst of our humanness.

When we experience physical limitations because of our embodiment and regular bodily needs, home provides the physical location where those needs can be met, because the triune God is also at home in our physical spaces.[9] In *No Home Like Place*, Leonard Hjalmarson writes, "We can't locate ourselves, much less find ourselves, apart from the places we inhabit."[10] The incarnation (God taking on flesh in Jesus Christ) and the Lord's Prayer (that God's kingdom come and God's will be done on earth) remind us that our work and ministry are not abstract concepts but are rooted in our physical reality.

Thus, tentmakers are encouraged to see the daily interactions and activities within the home as the provision of a rhythm where God will minister to them as well as through them. James Smith invites us to "be attentive to the rhythms and rituals that constitute the background hum of our families."[11] Because God is in the home, the morning rush, meal-preparation chaos, and even nighttime exhaustion are invitations for the infusion of the Lord's presence as sanctuary. Envisioning home through

---

7. Fitch, *Faithful Presence*, 24.

8. Fitch, *Faithful Presence*, 25.

9. This requires a broad understanding of place: "Place is more than a location, it is a meaningful integration of activity and persons within location" (McAlpine, *Sacred Space*, 128).

10. Hjalmarson, *No Home Like Place*, 46.

11. Smith, *What You Love*, 113.

three images of sanctuary—refuge, hospitality, and worship—can help tentmakers embrace the notion that home provides a place to integrate our embodiment with God's presence in our midst.

Home as Refuge

The first image of sanctuary is a place of refuge. Our home is a place where we are formed in the desires and practices that invite the coming of God's kingdom. Rather than defaulting to a hectic homelife, we can reflect upon and be intentional about how our homes might become a refuge—a place of safety, comfort, and hope for ourselves, our family, and our neighbors. Seeing our home as a refuge does not mean that it will always be tidy, quiet, and orderly. Rather, our home becomes a refuge because God's presence is acknowledged.

The home as refuge is important because God is recognized not as the subject or object of our ministry but as the source of our ministry. The psalmist reminds us that "God is our refuge and strength, a very present help" (Ps 46:1). When God is the source of ministry, the goals and means of ministry can be recalibrated. Rather than seeking balance and accomplishment, we discover God's life, goodness, and creativity as evidence of God's presence in our home. As Michael Gorman states, "The Gospel does not offer a narrow version of abundant life as either material or spiritual. It offers eschatological life, which is divine life."[12] John Ortberg cautions against our culture's emphasis on balance, because it "tends to carry with it the notion that we are trying to make our lives more manageable, more convenient, more pleasant."[13] Refuge does not mean that our lives will always be unbalanced; rather, refuge acknowledges that the Lord is able to cope with our already unbalanced lives so that we, along with our neighbors, can be offered refreshment and hope in the midst of the day's busyness. Marva Dawn offers a word of encouragement: "Remember the point is not how much we finish, but how open we are to letting the Lord's grace enter and work triunely through us."[14] In other words, a refuge is a place to experience God's presence as freedom from the constant burden of ministry.

---

12. Gorman, *Abide and Go*, 55.
13. Ortberg, *Life You've Always Wanted*, 191.
14. Dawn, *Sense of the Call*, 138.

A place to begin to reframe our home as a refuge might be through a home dedication or house blessing.[15] As we pray through each room, we invite God's presence to work to reshape our loves, our relationships, and our activities within that space. When our home is a refuge, others will also experience God's presence. For example, one day a neighbor girl walked into Marilyn's kitchen and exclaimed, "I like coming here. I call this the sunshine house." Because God is present, the tentmaker's home becomes a place of compassion for self and for others, a place of grace even in the midst of chaos or failure. Tentmakers are invited to envision their homes as places of refuge that embody the safety and freedom of sanctuary.

The Hospitable Home

Second, our homes can exhibit sanctuary as God's provision of hospitality. Christine Pohl writes, "When we view our homes as personal spaces that are simultaneously crucial to God's work in the world, . . . homes can become small outposts of God's kingdom."[16] In other words, the tentmaker's home becomes a living example of *shālōm*, revealing wholeness and harmony.[17] Counterculturally, we move away from entertaining to hospitality. Instead of experiencing the stress of extra cleaning required to make ourselves more presentable on Instagram, we invite people simply to come be with us in our homes (at least one research-project participant mentioned this stress). God's presence in the home means God serves as host to meet our needs and to serve our neighbors. As Dean Flemming writes, "Jesus followers not only experience God's *shalom*, they give it away."[18]

Being hospitable does not mean that our homes will always be full of people. But it does mean that others are invited to experience restoration

---

15. Several denominations, including Methodist, Anglican, and Catholic, include a ritual "blessing of the home" where congregants gather and pray through each room of the house in order to ask for God's blessing upon the home and the people within it. See The United Methodist Church, "Blessing of a Home"; the General Synod of the Anglican Church of Canada, "Occasional Celebrations."

16. Pohl, *Living into Community*, 170–71.

17. In reference to John 20:19, 21, 26, where Jesus says, "Peace be with you," Dean Flemming writes: "This peace—God's wide-ranging shalom—signifies more than simply a conventional greeting or a calm state of mind. In the context, it speaks of forgiveness of their failures, a restored relationship, and a freedom from the hostilities of others" (Flemming, *Why Mission?*, 63).

18. Flemming, *Why Mission?*, 63.

of relationships; those who were once strangers and enemies find common ground in order to become friends. Henri Nouwen defines hospitality as "the creation of a free space where the stranger can enter and become a friend instead of an enemy."[19] Tentmaking calls us to the revolutionary work of bringing change in our neighborhoods and cities. Parker Palmer reminds us that our private and public lives are related.[20] When we learn to share our resources and interact with the stranger in our private sphere, we become less anxious about scarcity and diversity in the public realm. As Palmer explains, "The simple fact of sharing creates a meaningful sense of abundance, that abundance which comes from knowing we do not stand alone or in constant competition with each other."[21] Reframing the home through the lens of sanctuary and hospitality reminds the tentmaker that God is the supplier of all that is needed for mission and ministry.

Home as a Place of Worship

Finally, the home serves as a sanctuary of worship. In *Liturgy of the Ordinary*, Tish Warren reflects upon how the mundane practices of ordinary daily life become practices of worship—not in spite of our physical limitations or regardless of our physicality but right in the midst of our humanness. She reflects on the goodness of creation, the value of our bodies, and the importance of the incarnation.[22] In fact, she states that "the body is not incidental to our faith, but integral to our worship."[23]

In our homes, we have daily routines. We make meals, sweep floors, do laundry, and read bedtime stories. No matter how much significance we feel at work or how troublesome the challenges of church, we will return home at the end of the day to brush our teeth and go to sleep. When God's presence infuses the routines of our humanness, we discover that our daily patterns have the potential to become reshaped as rituals of worship. Harrison Warren writes: "I often want to skip the boring, daily stuff to get to the thrill of an edgy faith. But it's in the dailiness of the Christian faith . . . that God's transformation takes root and grows."[24] When God's presence

---

19. Nouwen, *Reaching Out*, 71.
20. Palmer, *Company of Strangers*.
21. Palmer, *Company of Strangers*, 47.
22. Harrison Warren, *Liturgy of the Ordinary*, 38.
23. Harrison Warren, *Liturgy of the Ordinary*, 39.
24. Harrison Warren, *Liturgy of the Ordinary*, 36.

infuses our daily lives at home, we see these routines as opportunities for worship, as the reordered basis of mission. This integration of embodiment with divine reality points to the theological significance of the home as a place of worship.

Worship expresses our dependence upon God as the sustainer of life and of ministry. Being on mission is not about our ability to accomplish a task, build the church, or achieve success, but rather ministry itself is an expression of worship as we participate in what God is bringing forth in the world. Lesslie Newbigin provides this exhortation: "The one who has been called and loved by the Lord, will want to be where he is. . . . At the heart of mission is simply the desire to be with him and to give him the service of our lives."[25] When the tentmaker reframes the home to see God's presence there, the home becomes a sanctuary where daily routines become ritual expressions of our worship, reminding us that God is also the sustainer and completer of mission.[26]

Summary

Tentmakers experience busy home lives. Thus, they are tempted to see the activities at home as unimportant for, unrelated to, or even in competition with the responsibilities of employment and ministry. However, reframing the home as sanctuary provides a way for tentmakers to begin to integrate their differing spheres. When home is a place of refuge, the tentmaker acknowledges the Lord as the source of life, work, and ministry. When home is a place of hospitality, the tentmaker is reminded that God is the one who supplies necessary resources and serves as host to meet the needs of self, family, and neighbor. Finally, when home is a place of worship and the routines of daily life are expressions of worship, the tentmaker is reminded that the Lord is the sustainer and completer of mission. Ministry, argues Andrew Root, "correlates with God's own being."[27] The tentmaker still has much to undertake over the course of the day. However, reframing the home as sanctuary provides a way to theologically integrate life at home with mission in the world.

25. Newbigin, *Pluralist Society*, 127.
26. Draper, "Theological Reflections," 68.
27. Root, *Secular Age*, 174.

Questions for Reflection

1. What words would you use to describe your home? Have you walked through your home and invited God to come and dwell in these physical spaces?
2. What would it look like if your home were a sanctuary characterized by being a place of refuge, hospitality, and worship?
3. Brené Brown explains that "in our desperate search for joy in our lives we missed the memo. If we want to live a life of meaning and contribution, *we have to become intentional* about cultivating sleep and play. We have to let go of exhaustion, busyness, and productivity as status symbols and measures of self-worth."[28] How are you intentional in your approach to home?

Bibliography

Bickers, Dennis W. *The Art and Practice of Bivocational Ministry: A Pastor's Guide*. Kansas City: Beacon Hill, 2013.

Brown, Brené. *Dare to Lead: Brave Work. Tough Conversations. Whole Hearts.* New York: Random House, 2018.

Dawn, Marva J. *The Sense of the Call*. Grand Rapids: Eerdmans, 2006.

Draper, Marilyn. "Theological Reflections of a Veteran Church Planter." *Witness: Journal of the Academy for Evangelism in Theological Education* 27 (2013) 57–82. https://journals.sfu.ca/witness/index.php/witness/issue/viewIssue/3/3.

Flemming, Dean. *Why Mission? Reframing New Testament Theology*. Nashville: Abingdon, 2015.

Fitch, David E. *Faithful Presence: Seven Disciplines That Shape the Church for Mission*. Downers Grove, IL: InterVarsity, 2016.

The General Synod of the Anglican Church of Canada. "Occasional Celebrations of the Anglican Church of Canada." Toronto: ABC, 1992. https://www.anglican.ca/wp-content/uploads/OccasionalCelebrations.pdf.

Gorman, Michael J. *Abide and Go*. Eugene, OR: Wipf & Stock, 2018.

Harrison Warren, Tish. *Liturgy of the Ordinary*. Downers Grove, IL: InterVarsity, 2016.

Hjalmarson, Leonard. *No Home Like Place: A Christian Theology of Place*. 2nd ed. Portland: Urban Loft, 2015.

McAlpine, William R. *Sacred Space for the Missional Church*. Eugene, OR: Wipf & Stock, 2011.

Newbigin, Lesslie. *The Gospel in a Pluralist Society*. Grand Rapids: Eerdmans, 1989.

Nouwen, Henri J. M. *Reaching Out: The Three Movements of the Spiritual Life*. Garden City, NY: Image, 1986.

---

28. Brown, *Dare to Lead*, 106; italics added.

Ortberg, John. *The Life You've Always Wanted*. Grand Rapids: Zondervan, 1997.
Palmer, Parker J. *The Company of Strangers*. New York: Crossroad, 1981.
Pohl, Christine D. *Living into Community: Cultivating Practices That Sustain Us*. Grand Rapids: Eerdmans, 2012.
Root, Andrew. *The Pastor in a Secular Age*. Grand Rapids: Baker Academic, 2019.
Smith, James K. A. *You Are What You Love: The Spiritual Power of Habit*. Grand Rapids: Brazos, 2016.
Swinton, John. *Practical Theology and Qualitative Research Methods*. London: SCM, 2006.
The United Methodist Church. "A Service for the Blessing of a Home." Abingdon, 1992. https://www.umcdiscipleship.org/book-of-worship/a-service-for-the-blessing-of-a-home.
Watson, James W., and Narry F. Santos. "Tentmaking: Creative Mission Opportunities within a Secularizing Canadian Society." In *Mission and Evangelism in a Secularizing World*, edited by Narry F. Santos and Mark Naylor, 131–32. Eugene, OR: Pickwick, 2019.

6

Sabbath Rest in Multivocational Ministry

Mark D. Chapman

THERE IS CONSIDERABLE DIVERSITY in how multivocational leaders organize their lives to make them feasible. Diversity of work and ministry responsibilities, family situations, and incomes leads to many different configurations of this approach to ministry. Nonetheless, all is not well. Multivocational leaders express concerns about boundaries, home-life balance, time-management strategies, and getting time for rest and renewal.[1] Many have developed an approach to rest and renewal to deal with these concerns that includes a biblical Sabbath. This chapter uses the actual experiences of multivocational leaders from the Canadian Multivocational Ministry Project (CMMP) to identify the challenges and possibilities of Sabbath as a practical practice for the rest and renewal of these leaders.

Sabbath and the Life of the Multivocational Minister

God provides very few rules for the Sabbath—only simple guidelines: "rest, cease from work, celebrate, remember, observe, deny yourself, delight yourself."[2] Sabbath, found in the fourth commandment in Exod 20:8–11 and Deut 5:12–15, has two main components: cessation of work and

1. Watson et al., *Canadian Multivocational Ministry Project*.
2. Buchanan, *Rest of God*, 111.

celebrating a day to the Lord.³ The two components are interrelated: the day is sanctified, in part, by stopping work. The aim of the commandment is the well-being of individuals specifically and society generally. Part of that well-being comes from getting a rest from work. It is a ceasing of work for everyone and thus has a justice component related to how we treat our neighbors.⁴ Sabbath aims to draw us into community and signifies the community's relationship with God.⁵ The Sabbath is a day specifically set aside to celebrate that all time is God's.⁶ Buchanan describes Sabbath as a day and as an attitude.⁷ As Heschel notes, "It is not an interlude but the climax of living," and it is not for frivolity but for comfort, pleasure, and celebration.⁸

Sabbath is not optional but rather is a fundamental ritual for living a godly life.⁹ The Sabbath contributes to God's purposes of making his people holy and demonstrates dependence on God.¹⁰ It keeps us from thinking that we control what is going on around us by showing us "our irrelevance and our dependence."¹¹ Celebrating Sabbath keeps us from idolizing our own work. It helps us "to think and care about the God who created us and God's work, about God's plan and our place in it."¹² It is a gift and a blessing as much as it is a command by God.¹³ In Sabbath, we encounter means of addressing our problems because our actions reflect God's creation design and thus establish life patterns that are open to God's work.¹⁴

---

3. Miller, *Ten Commandments*, 119, 130.
4. Miller, *Ten Commandments*, 122, 127; Swoboda, *Subversive Sabbath*, 90–91.
5. Swoboda, *Subversive Sabbath*, 67; Miller, *Ten Commandments*, 153.
6. Heschel, *Sabbath*; Swoboda, *Subversive Sabbath*.
7. Buchanan, *Rest of God*, 4.
8. Heschel, *Sabbath*, 14, 17–18.
9. Miller, *Ten Commandments*, 151. See also Exod 31:14.
10. Harrison, *NLT Study Bible*, note on Exod 31:12–18.
11. Buchanan, *Rest of God*, 87, Swoboda, *Subversive Sabbath*, 181.
12. Miller, *Ten Commandments*, 133.
13. Miller, *Ten Commandments*, 122–23, 126.
14. Smith, *What You Love*; Miller, *Ten Commandments*, 131. See also Smith, *Desiring the Kingdom*.

PART 3 | ISSUES ARISING FROM MULTIVOCATIONAL MINISTRY

Challenges to Sabbath Rest

Multivocational leaders interviewed for the CMMP recognize the need to counteract the stress of the multivocational life. They recognize overwork and busyness and take steps to respond to it. They identify the high stakes of ministry and realize that rest and renewal are necessary to sustain effective ministry. They are also mostly conscious of the effect of multivocational ministry on their families and have strategies to mitigate any negative effects that their families might experience (see chapter 5).

Ministry Stressors and Multivocational Ministry

Multivocational leaders need to engage in rest and renewal because ministry can be stressful (see chapter 2). The mundane stressors of ministry work discussed in the literature, such as being overwhelmed with work, guilt, switching costs, complexity, and the perceived high stakes of the job are also of concern for multivocational leaders.[15]

Working long hours is not necessarily a problem. However, feeling overwhelmed by workload, feeling like one cannot take a break, and unrewarding work are problems.[16] Relentless busyness can be productive, but it can also be harmful.[17] Proeschold-Bell et al. found that issues like life unpredictability and guilt about not doing enough contribute to clergy anxiety.[18] Clergy often have many demands on their time that compete for their attention.[19] Proeschold-Bell and Byassee explain that "toggling from task to task can be harder on someone than doing the same very stressful task all day."[20] Pastoral work has many such "switching costs," and this can be "stressful and exhausting" over the long term.[21] To this complexity and

---

15. Hough et al., "Relationships"; Proeschold-Bell and Byassee, *Faithful and Fractured*; Proeschold-Bell et al., "Effort-Reward Imbalance Theory." These stressors were chosen to illustrate the experiences of multivocational leaders and should not be taken as a comprehensive or representative description of clergy stress.

16. Proeschold-Bell and Byassee, *Faithful and Fractured*, 3.

17. Koessler, *Radical Pursuit of Rest*, 17–34; Williams, *Stand Out*.

18. Proeschold-Bell et al., "Effort-Reward Imbalance Theory."

19. Proeschold-Bell and Byassee, *Faithful and Fractured*, 27. The problem here appears to be the large number of demands, not loss of control, which is a primary problem in other occupations (Proeschold-Bell and Byassee, *Faithful and Fractured*, 28).

20. Proeschold-Bell and Byassee, *Faithful and Fractured*, 2.

21. Bloom, *Flourishing in Ministry*, 23–24; Monsell, "Task Switching."

diversity is added the high stakes of ministry work, which is punctuated with the unexpected and has "little structure or guidance for prioritizing ministry work."[22] The understanding of such work as sacred to both clergy and congregation also increases stress levels.[23]

Challenges of Multivocational Ministry

Such challenges can be exacerbated in multivocational ministry because they combine the regular challenges of ministry with the diverse demands and additional challenges of navigating multiple work settings. Overwork, switching costs, guilt, complexity, and high stakes are challenges for multivocational leaders—even if not unique to them.

In the CMMP, some multivocational leaders reported that they work more than they want to or had not anticipated how much work multivocational responsibilities would be. One participant talked about taking over three years to recover from burnout. Others talked of the challenge of taking time for renewal. Such challenges relate, in part, to the multiple demands on the life of the multivocational minister. Respondents had a lot to say about the effect of the time demands of multivocational ministry on their home lives. Family life, while it did not always rise to the level of explicit guilt, was a common area of expressed concern. The busyness of this life could lead to missed vacations, and spouses sometimes ended up with more of the housework. Multivocational leaders talk of overcoming the guilt of not being able to do everything and of the need to set boundaries so that one part of their life does not take over another. Some wondered about the challenges their children experienced; one described the effect of their lifestyle on their family as "horrible."[24] Some of this was the result of what one participant called "an administrative toll that's paid the more complex your work schedule is." Complexity meant that sometimes spouses could not get time off or vacation together. It could also mean that leaders work long hours and have to make trade-offs in how they spend their time and

22. Bloom, *Flourishing in Ministry*, 22–25.

23. Proeschold-Bell and Byassee, *Faithful and Fractured*, 16. For example, sanctification theory argues that when something is perceived to be sacred, individuals will exert energy toward it, it will foster strong emotions, and its loss can be devastating (see Pargament and Mahoney, "Sacred Matters," 179–98; Proeschold-Bell and Byassee, *Faithful and Fractured*, 17–25).

24. For more details about the effects of multivocational ministry on homelife, see chapter 5 in this volume.

who they spend their time with. This complexity sometimes catches them by surprise: "I didn't realize how busy it was going to end up feeling; even if it's not a number of hours, it's just that your brain is on one thing, and then your brain has to be on something else." Many need flexible job schedules to accommodate complexity, yet these leaders feel called by God to the specific ministries and sometimes the specific combination of jobs they have. This makes what they do high stakes, because it is not just a way of earning a living or passing the time but rather something that God "wants" them to do (see chapter 2 for further reflection on these issues).

Sabbath Rest and the Multivocational Leader

Given these challenges, there is a clear need for multivocational ministers to engage in renewal activities as a response to stress, but more importantly, to develop the resilience they need to cope with challenges when they arrive. Yet, when we look at what people actually do, it can be hard to distinguish between simple time off and a biblical Sabbath. This is the difference between activities that involve taking a break from work without a specific agenda (time off) and those activities that feed into people so that they have spiritual resources for living (Sabbath). Sabbath renewal is about the restoration of one's soul for the work of the ministry. Sabbath brings rest and renewal into conscious alignment with God's purposes.

While the practice of Sabbath is not a panacea for all that stresses pastors, it is one of the most prominent historical practices for developing a healthy approach to life, is accessible to people in ministry, and is something that was addressed by thirty-five of forty participants in the CMMP.[25] Multivocational ministers have to come up with strategies to mitigate their challenges and get rest and renewal. Sabbath shapes the leader so they have the means to cope with challenges practically rather than just responding emotionally. It draws people into community, which is an opportunity to develop deep relationships and reduce isolation, which, in turn, helps prevent stress symptoms.[26]

---

25. This is striking because the CMMP did not necessarily ask specifically about rest and renewal. A question about how work life is arranged included the probing question "Where do you find rest and renewal in your week?" There were no specific questions or prompts that asked about Sabbath.

26. Proeschold-Bell and Byassee make three suggestions for preventing stress symptoms: "Try to engage in problem-solving coping, not just emotion-focused coping . . . cultivate at least two relationships in which you can bare your soul . . . [and] avoid social

What Time Off Looks Like for Multivocational Leaders

Time off can be positive even if it is not Sabbath. The CMMP identified activities that were time off from work and aimed at some kind of renewal. The most mentioned renewal activity was exercise, followed by spending time at home. Other popular activities involved socializing and time in nature (e.g., gardening, hiking). People also mentioned baking, travel, community theater, and writing. Some activities were presented as self-soothing: walking the dog, watching sports, vegging out, or time at the bar with friends. Activities that were more entertainment focused included TV, movies, watching Netflix, and sports. These appear to be exclusively time off, but the role of entertainment activities was complicated. One mother found watching TV was a restful time with her children. Other claimed renewal activities sounded a lot like hard work (e.g., hosting a radio program).[27] Sometimes individuals were not quite sure these activities qualified as renewal.

Identifying activities as taking time off should not be understood as a criticism of these ministers. Stopping work for something else is a core feature of Sabbath. However, such activities on their own may not bring the restoration ministers need, because while they may bring rest, they do not necessarily equip them with the spiritual resources for life they need to thrive in ministry specifically and life generally.

Practicing Sabbath

Multivocational leaders' descriptions of getting rest and renewal show that they practice both cessation of work and a day to the Lord aimed at aligning themselves with God's purposes.

Cessation of Work

Many CMMP participants talked about Sabbath as a literal day on which they try not to work. Monday was the most commonly mentioned day, but Thursday, Saturday, Sunday, and Friday were all mentioned as Sabbath days.

---

isolation at all costs" (*Faithful and Fractured*, 74). Sabbath has the potential to contribute here.

27. This individual loves music, and so hosting a community radio show meant that they had regular time to just enjoy music.

Sometimes respondents indicated that their Sabbath day moved around or that times of rest and renewal were "feast or famine." Respondents protected Sabbath in a variety of different ways (such as not running errands, answering the phone, or checking email). Others did not specifically identify a Sabbath but did have days where they tried not to work. However, sometimes Sabbath depended on what else was going on; it could be delayed or missed.

> So, Monday can sometimes be a Sabbath and my day off, and sometimes it's a day where I get visiting done . . . It is the day I slot other things into. And so, if I'm reading or visiting or have an appointment in a city to make or something [like] that, Monday is the day it gets done.

A main objective for not working was to get rest. Activities included exercise, walking, getting extra sleep, baking, spending time with family or in nature, spiritual direction, and watching TV. Here, we see a fair bit of overlap with time off. Some respondents specifically identified how these activities were renewing and thus might be Sabbath. Others just seemed to list things they were doing when they were not working with no specific mention of their attitude to these activities or their end goal. Descriptions like these made Sabbath seem less like an opportunity to reencounter God and more like a break from work, even if they were specifically identified as Sabbath.

A Day to the Lord

The second broad category of Sabbath is a "day to the Lord." Three areas where this can be seen in multivocational lives include Sabbath as a theological category, references to spiritual activities, and activities specifically identified as related to spiritual renewal.

The first category of references to Sabbath were those that were explicitly theological. One participant referenced "thinking of the concept of the Sabbath," and another mentioned incorporating the Sabbath as part of a "rule of life." Sabbath was mentioned as a theological necessity and as finding "rhythms of connecting with God in the deeper sense that God is inviting us to." It was also identified as counterclultural because rest can be understood as unproductive. Sometimes, individuals mentioned Sabbath but provided no details about what they meant.

Unsurprisingly, there was a fair amount of reference to spiritual activities. Prayer was a common response to a question about renewal. One respondent mentioned spending ten to fifteen minutes in prayer with their spouse each morning. Another talked about getting fifteen minutes of prayer here and there throughout the day. Yet another talked of the common Christian practice of a morning devotional time. Other spiritual practices mentioned included working with a spiritual director, discernment, healthy rhythms, and centering prayer. Some highlighted the need for daily time with God or talked about how their work allowed times of prayerfulness and contemplation.

Other renewal activities that were not directly connected to spiritual practice but provided spiritual restoration included spending time in nature and with family or friends or just slowing down for a morning. Some of the activities mentioned were also episodic, such as the request for a sabbatical, taking a day away, or going on a silent retreat.

The Challenge of Keeping the Sabbath

This description of renewal activities shows that multivocational leaders are involved in many activities that could be reasonably understood as a biblical Sabbath but also many whose end is more ambiguous. Keeping the Sabbath is challenging. Some participants valued having a non-workday without indicating that they actually had one or identified the challenge of actually taking one. Others lamented "not keeping a Sabbath day" and indicated that if "finances weren't an issue," they would have a Sabbath day. Some said they were not getting one. One respondent did not think the idea of a Sabbath day was necessary and made a theological argument against this idea but was careful to explain that they valued rest. Most of our respondents found some way to incorporate something they called Sabbath into their week.

Yet, sometimes the discussion of renewal activities pointed at a busyness that made renewal hard. The individual who indicated they prayed fifteen to twenty minutes at a time said they had no larger time slots. Other respondents specifically mentioned a lack in this area (e.g., a respondent who said they needed to "find more spaciousness for my spiritual life"). Another individual said they got time for relaxation on their day off only 75 percent of the time. Exercise sometimes consisted of walking to work. Some frankly indicated that this was an area of struggle. Renewal activities like days off were more complicated in families where it was hard to find days off together. Others talked about times of rest and renewal as seasonal.

Summary: Why Multivocational Leaders Need More Than Time Off

Exodus advocates keeping the Sabbath because God rested on the seventh day. Deuteronomy calls for keeping the Sabbath because of having been rescued from slavery. Miller identifies this difference as modeling God versus celebrating freedom.[28] The key point is that in neither case is keeping the Sabbath about doing nothing or aimless time off. The difference is between an activity that aims to distract from work and one that aims to engage us with life by celebrating the freedom of living a life modeled after God. Time off is what Mark Buchanan called "a vacation—literally, a vacating, an evacuation."[29] Eugene Peterson more colorfully talks about an illegitimate Sabbath.[30] Just doing something different from work will not provide the resources multivocational leaders need for continued ministry, nor will it be the "the climax of living."[31] Sabbath is a filling and a time of refreshing.[32] One should stop working but also aim toward the end of knowing God better.

CMMP participants had a lot to say about rest and renewal. They understood the need to take some time away from work, but not all of them practiced Sabbath. A large variety of activities were considered renewal. Almost everybody got the idea of taking a day off, although not all of them practiced it, and many mentioned aspects of life that might intervene. The second half of the concept of Sabbath, a day to the Lord, was much less commonly practiced. There were those that seem to know something of Sabbath. These individuals talked about the freedom to not be "productive"—being rather than doing. In addition, there was a fair bit of mention

---

28. Miller, *Ten Commandments*, 124–30.
29. Buchanan, *Rest of God*, 35.
30. Peterson, *Pastor*, 220.
31. Heschel, *Sabbath*, 14. It is also possible that just taking time off could cause, rather than relieve, problems. We now recognize that excessive distractions and amusements (e.g., social media, binge-watching videos, incessant newsfeed scrolling) can be signs of overwork and stress (see Williams, *Stand Out*; Borgmann, *Power Failure*). Swoboda explains that "we have replaced Sabbath with a kind of therapeutic individualism that seeks to self-entertain, self-please, self-soothe" (*Subversive Sabbath*, 20).
32. Buchanan, *Rest of God*, 36.

of regular spiritual practices (e.g., devotions, prayer, reading, meditation, silence, music, walking). Yet, for many multivocational ministers, they are only getting half of Sabbath because they are only practicing half of the theological concept—they do not get a whole day off, or they do not understand the spiritual-renewal side of Sabbath. It is possible to practice Sabbath as a multivocational leader, but it is challenging. It requires intentionality but could also benefit from external support (e.g., finances, childcare, expressed permission).[33] Multivocational leaders need support to help them set aside a specific day and protect it vigorously, take into account the needs and schedules of the whole family, dedicate time for spiritually renewing activities, find people to take on ministry tasks, and get relief from demands to overwork. Sabbath will not look the same for every multivocational leader, but it is necessary, and it is possible.

Questions for Reflection

1. Do you and the leaders you work with get a Sabbath or just time off? How do you know?
2. What are your specific challenges that make taking a Sabbath difficult? What has to change to facilitate the regular practice of a Sabbath?
3. Buchanan says that "Sabbath's golden rule [is] *Cease from what is necessary. Embrace that which gives life.* And then do whatever you want."[34] What does this look like in practice?

Bibliography

Bickers, Dennis W. *The Art and Practice of Bivocational Ministry: A Pastor's Guide.* Kansas City: Beacon Hill, 2013.
Bloom, Matthew C. *Flourishing in Ministry: How to Cultivate Clergy Well-Being.* Lanham, MD: Rowman & Littlefield, 2019.
Borgmann, Albert. *Power Failure: Christianity in the Culture of Technology.* Grand Rapids: Brazos, 2003.
Buchanan, Mark. *The Rest of God: Restoring Your Soul by Restoring Sabbath.* Nashville: Thomas Nelson, 2006.
Burns, Bob, et al. *Resilient Ministry: What Pastors Told Us about Surviving and Thriving.* Downers Grove, IL: InterVarsity, 2012.

33. Buchanan, *Rest of God,* 129.
34. Buchanan, *Rest of God,* 129; italics in the original.

PART 3 | ISSUES ARISING FROM MULTIVOCATIONAL MINISTRY

Crary, David. "Stresses Multiply for Many Us Clergy: 'We Need Help Too.'" *The Associated Press*, Feb 18, 2020.
Harrison, Sean A., ed. *NLT Study Bible: New Living Translation*. Carol Stream, IL: Tyndale House, 2017.
Heschel, Abraham Joshua. *The Sabbath: Its Meaning for Modern Man*. New York: Farrar, Straus & Giroux, 2000.
Hough, Holly, et al. "Relationships between Sabbath Observance and Mental, Physical, and Spiritual Health in Clergy." *Pastoral Psychology* 68 (2019) 171–93. https://doi.org/10.1007/s11089-018-0838-9.
Koessler, John. *The Radical Pursuit of Rest: Escaping the Productivity Trap*. Downers Grove, IL: InterVarsity, 2016. EBook.
Malcolm, Wanda M., et al. "Measuring Ministry-Specific Stress and Satisfaction: The Psychometric Properties of the Positive and Negative Aspects Inventories." *Journal of Psychology and Theology* 47 (2019) 313–27. https://doi.org/10.1177/0091647119837018.
Meisenhelder, Janice Bell, and John P. Marcum. "Responses of Clergy to 9/11: Posttraumatic Stress, Coping, and Religious Outcomes." *Journal for the Scientific Study of Religion* 43 (2004) 547–54. https://www.jstor.org/stable/3590577.
Miller, Patrick D. *The Ten Commandments*. Louisville: Westminster John Knox, 2009.
Monsell, Stephen. "Task Switching." *Trends in Cognitive Sciences* 7 (2003) 134–40. https://doi.org/10.1016/s1364-6613(03)00028-7.
Olson, Richard P., et al. *A Guide to Ministry Self-Care: Negotiating Today's Challenges with Resilience and Grace*. Lanham, MD: Rowman & Littlefield, 2018.
Pargament, Kenneth I., and Annette Mahoney. "Sacred Matters: Sanctification as a Vital Topic for the Psychology of Religion." *International Journal for the Psychology of Religion* 15 (2005) 179–98. https://doi.org/10.1207/s15327582ijpr1503_1.
Peterson, Eugene H. *The Pastor: A Memoir*. New York: HarperOne, 2011.
Proeschold-Bell, Rae Jean, and Jason Byassee. *Faithful and Fractured: Responding to the Clergy Health Crisis*. Grand Rapids: Baker Academic, 2018.
Proeschold-Bell, Rae Jean, et al. "Using Effort-Reward Imbalance Theory to Understand High Rates of Depression and Anxiety among Clergy." *Journal of Primary Prevention* 34 (2013) 439–53. https://doi.org/10.1007/s10935-013-0321-4.
Scazzero, Peter. *The Emotionally Healthy Leader*. Grand Rapids: Zondervan, 2015.
———. *Emotionally Healthy Spirituality: Unleash a Revolution in Your Life in Christ*. Nashville: Thomas Nelson, 2011.
Scazzero, Peter, and Warren Bird. *The Emotionally Healthy Church*. Grand Rapids: Zondervan, 2003.
Searby, Mark A. *The Resilient Pastor: Ten Principles for Developing Pastoral Resilience*. Eugene, OR: Wipf & Stock, 2015.
Smith, James K. A. *Desiring the Kingdom: Worship, Worldview, and Cultural Formation*. Grand Rapids: Baker Academic, 2009.
———. *You Are What You Love: The Spiritual Power of Habit*. Grand Rapids: Brazos, 2016.
Steinke, Peter L. *Congregational Leadership in Anxious Times: Being Calm and Courageous No Matter What*. Lanham, MD: Rowman & Littlefield, 2014.
Swoboda, A. J. *Subversive Sabbath: The Surprising Power of Rest in a Nonstop World*. Grand Rapids: Brazos, 2018.

Vaccarino, Franco, and Tony (Max Anthony) Gerritsen. "Exploring Clergy Self-Care: A New Zealand Study." *The International Journal of Religion and Spirituality in Society* 3 (2013) 69–80. https://doi.org/10.18848/2154-8633/CGP/v03i02/59264.

Watson, James W., et al. *Canadian Multivocational Ministry Project: Research Report.* 2020. https://www.canadianmultivocationalministry.ca/report.

Williams, James. *Stand Out of Our Light.* Cambridge: Cambridge University Press, 2018.

7

Tending to the Tentmakers

Jared Siebert

> I hope that we can see bivocational ministry as a gift, rather than as the downfall of the church or whatever it is. I think . . . I think ministers are going to preach better. I think they're going to have a better understanding of "lay people." And I think that they'll have a better understanding of the world that surrounds them if they have a view that's outside the church. And I think . . . I think bivocational ministry is a gift rather than a deficit for the church.[1]

TENTMAKING IS NOTHING NEW. It has been a part of life in the Christian community since our very earliest beginnings. The fact that we have to remind ourselves that tentmaking is a normal part of how churches are led is a peculiar artifact of Christendom. As Christendom enters its twilight years, we are now re-recognizing the practice of tentmaking. This is far from a problem and far from a sign of decline. It is a return to normal. It is an opportunity to re-harness the very tangible but recently forgotten benefits and opportunities that come with tentmaking. Our task in this time is not to cope with tentmaking or devise strategies to make it go away. Our task is to tend to the tentmakers among us so that we can reap the benefits and rewards this mode of pastoral leadership offers.

So, how do we tend to the tentmakers? To answer this question, we need to consider the opportunities and challenges that tentmaking creates

---

1. Quote from Canadian Multivocational Ministry Project interviewee.

at three different levels: the personal/pastoral level, the local-church level, and the denominational level.

Personal/Pastoral Level

The first level we need to tend to is the personal. Tentmaking's greatest gifts and most significant challenges are first and foremost personal. The life of the tentmaker is the primary arena in which the pressures, expectations, and possibilities emerge. If tentmaking is going well or not so well, it is felt at this level first. Because of this, we need to pay particular attention to opportunities and challenges in the life of the tentmaker. The opportunities that emerged from our research included wider spaces to establish identity, free and honest attachment to their role, the ability to make bolder moves in leadership, and a deeper theological appreciation for integrated living. The challenges of tentmaking were in the areas of managing expectations, the logistical challenges of finding work-life balance, and the challenges of establishing times of rest.

Opportunities

Many of the participants in our study saw tentmaking as a positive factor in their sense of self. They reported a greater sense of personal freedom and felt less prone to building their entire identity around "being a pastor." This was tentmaking's greatest gift to them:

> (M)inisters are captured by congregations. Their work is there. Their faith life is there. Their family is there.... They're just totally enfolded into a congregation. And I think it will be part of the beauty of [tentmaking] ministry... the church realizes that you're not just the church's—you're also, you know, you have another life.

A few others noted that this greater sense of freedom and identity outside of being a pastor enabled them to be more truthful in their preaching and in their dealings with congregation members.

There are at least two factors responsible for this. The first is economic. Tentmakers do not derive their entire income from just one place. In many cases, tentmakers had several sources of income, and in some cases, the church made up less than half of the tentmaker's salary. In a few instances, the pastoral role was voluntary. Why is this significant? Put plainly, economics can play a role in the kinds of decisions pastors make. The temptation to soften truths or to ignore problems can be exacerbated when they are tied to one's livelihood. Tentmaking offers a unique chance to be more free—or, in some cases, entirely free—from the influence of economics on pastoral ministry.

A second factor in the tentmaker's greater sense of freedom flows from how they construct their personal identity. Several of our tentmakers expressed that they felt free to construct their identity around roles other than being a pastor. Why is this also significant? If one's identity and self-worth are entirely founded on being a local church pastor, there are temptations to lead the church in a more risk-averse way. Unpopular but necessary ministry directions or engaging in difficult missional ventures could be seen as too risky if one's identity is tied solely to being a pastor. Whether or not these wider spaces of economic freedom and identity construction are actual or simply based on perception is inconsequential. Perception is reality. Feeling freer to make tough ministry calls is what matters here. Freedom creates new possibilities. What would change in the church and in the overall job satisfaction of pastors if they felt they were able to be more honest in their dealings? What would change if more pastors felt they were able to take greater risks? What could change if pastors felt freer to pursue unpopular or difficult missional endeavors? Well, the good news is that the Canadian church is about to find out. As tentmaking is increasingly normalized in the Canadian church, we will get to see firsthand the benefits of this perception/reality.

A number of the participants in the study reported that tentmaking enabled them to live in a more theologically integrated way:

> For me, that means ensuring that different aspects of life are incorporated, and I'm thinking back to now like "God in My Everything"; just this whole idea that life, all of life, is infused with God and no matter what part it is, we can see him, find him, notice him, and we can worship him . . .

Several also noted that their tentmaking arrangement was fertile ground for preaching and for developing a more nuanced understanding of the people in their congregations. Again, whether or not these benefits are actual or perceived, it is good news for tentmakers, the local church, and the broader church in Canada.

Challenges

Tentmaking ministry is not all sunshine and rainbows. There are also distinct challenges to sustaining this kind of arrangement at the personal level. Making tentmaking sustainable and emotionally healthy means wrestling with and making peace with a myriad of expectations: balancing life and work, overall performance of tasks in all forms of employment, a healthy sense of calling and satisfaction, and even whether or not tentmaking damages the overall health and vitality of their congregation. All of these expectations have to be wrestled with. Complicating things further, tentmakers reported these expectations came from many different angles: from the self, from within the family unit (spouses and children), from within the local church, and even from other colleagues and denominational leaders. If we are to tend to the tentmaker, they must be aided and trained as they work out a healthy relationship with various expectations. They must be given resources that help make the expectations reasonable, clear, and concrete. Anything less would make them unmanageable. Sustainable and healthy tentmaking involves actively identifying, coping with, adjusting, and revising expectations. Damaging tentmaking means being overwhelmed by a pervasive sense of failure in several, if not all, of these areas of life. Tending to the tentmakers will require a concerted and multidimensional effort from within the heart of the tentmaker, from within the family unit, from within the local congregation, and from within the broader clergy. This is no simple task, and the Canadian church is only at the beginning stages of understanding these issues. More research and training are needed to better understand the power, source, and effect of expectations on tentmakers.

Tentmaking is not simply battling elusive ideas like expectations; there are gritty and real logistical challenges as well. Complicating matters, there is no one-size-fits-all option for working through the logistics. Tentmaking can mean taking on various vocational demands that are seasonal, weekly or monthly, or entirely unpredictable and erratic. Our time study of tentmakers revealed that tending to tentmakers requires assisting tentmakers in establishing an individualized plan.[2]

Another point of personal challenge and concern for tentmakers was finding a regular rhythm for Sabbath. This was alarmingly common among our participants. We know that rest is vital to all life on earth. It is also

---

2. Watson et al., *Canadian Multivocational Ministry Project*. See Appendix 3 of the report (pp. 32–35) for examples of weekly schedules.

vital to the pattern of life God established. Because of this, rest needs to be central when constructing a time-management strategy for tentmakers. One participant put it this way: "Sabbath, it's easy to not set today aside for rest. So, I think it is in establishing a rhythm, looking at the components of life that are not to be missed and finding a way to incorporate them." Once again, our time study did not reveal a single day of the week that worked for all tentmakers. Each tentmaking arrangement required time to work out a unique balance and rhythm. Many of the more sustainable tentmaking arrangements in our study appeared to be years in the making. In our tending to tentmakers, we should expect that finding the right balance will take careful, patient, and consistent vigilance.

Local-Church Level

Tentmaking is not a solo mission. It involves and impacts many important dimensions of the local church. Proper tending to tentmakers will require local churches to actively embrace the unique opportunities and overcome the unique challenges that tentmaking creates for their lives together. Local churches, if they are to receive the benefits of tentmaking, will need to embrace tentmaking's unique gift of an enhanced sense of the "priesthood of all believers" and the chance to actively work out robust theologies. Local churches will also need to actively wrestle with the challenges of collectively managing group expectations and finding enough people to continue the work of the local church.

Opportunities

Tentmaking has a lot to offer the local church. Apart from its obvious economic advantages, there are other gifts it offers. Tentmakers, especially those with stable and sustainable arrangements, noted that their congregants were more apt to step into larger and more demanding roles than would otherwise be the case in churches with univocational leadership. It is common for laypeople to step into larger roles and discover new gifts in themselves than would have been considered with a full-time pastor present. In churches where tentmaking is the norm, these larger roles and newly discovered gifts remain a permanent part of the way the church regularly operates. Tentmaking offers not only greater freedom for pastors to establish identities and financial means *outside* the church, it also allows lay leaders to develop identities *inside* the church. Tending to the tentmakers involves paying careful attention to the way in which responsibilities, ministries, and work inside and outside the church are divided. This process will not only go a long way to making the tentmaker's life possible, it will also allow for congregants to discover and develop their giftings.

The very process of making tentmaking possible encouraged local churches to develop clearer and more jointly held theologies, sometimes inadvertently. We noted in some cases that robust understandings of work, ecclesiology, the nature and role of the pastor, and the nature and role of the laity were expressed by the leaders of these churches. As tentmakers and local leaders worked out the practical issues (scheduling, prioritizing energy investment, managing congregational expectations, and offering new opportunities for laypeople), the process yielded a collective and intentional sifting of the nature, the function, and the purpose of the church. What resulted was a more robust and collectively held set of theological insights. While few of the project participants articulated a novel vision of the church, what they did have was a collection of theological insights that were held not only by the tentmaker but by the broader congregation as well. Life-giving and pragmatic theology is vitally important to the health of the local church and the broader Canadian church. As the broader church struggles with its ongoing role in the Canadian context, it is worth noting that local churches (intentionally engaging in tentmaking) are unique sources of theological innovation and insight.

Challenges

Tentmaking creates challenges for the local church whether this arrangement is chosen out of necessity or purposeful intent. The work of managing expectations is of primary importance to the work of tentmaking in the local church. If we are to properly tend to the tentmakers among us, careful and active work needs to go into identifying, coping with, adjusting, and revising expectations of various congregational members. To do this well, tentmakers, their families, local church leaders, and even denominational leaders each have an important role to play. Each of these groups can either threaten or enhance the stability and sustainability of the tentmaking arrangement. It is important for the Canadian church to begin developing training materials that specifically address tentmaking. We see this book as a helpful first step. However, further research and investment are required if we are to do this well.

All local churches experience the challenge of finding enough people to carry on the work. Churches that choose tentmaking are no exception. The scope of our research was unable to make a clear determination of whether tentmaking makes this challenge particularly acute in tentmaking churches. We simply note that this is a struggle for tentmaking churches as well.

Denominational Level

Our final level to consider is that of the broader church. The attendant opportunities and challenges that tentmaking affords extend far beyond the personal and local-church levels and impact our collective experience in denominational families and the broader Canadian church. The opportunities tentmaking offers us are a path forward for sustainable mission in Canada and expanding mission opportunities into new areas of Canadian culture. Just like the other levels, there are attendant challenges as well. Tentmaking poses unique challenges to denominations in the areas of training and maintaining wider group cohesion.

Opportunities

As the church in Canada continues to wrestle with the rise of what Charles Taylor calls the "secular age,"[3] tentmaking offers the broader church several new possibilities for sustainability. As has already been noted, tentmaking is an economically viable mode of operating. As church sizes continue to contract, so will our economic means. Thus, tentmaking will increasingly become a solid "go-to" option when times are tight. Secondly, as mentioned above, the sifting process (at the personal and local-church levels) that intentional tentmaking requires can often lead to more streamlined churches. Tentmakers and tentmaking churches are vital conversation partners as the broader Canadian church does its own sifting work amid the changing realities of modern life in Canada. Tentmaking churches are not simply a problem to solve or manage. They are not a sign of failure or trouble. They are sources of immense creativity, possibilities, and theological insights.

3. Taylor, *Secular Age*.

Tentmaking churches are uniquely poised to offer insights into our ongoing collective mission into new areas of Canadian culture. Their most obvious contribution to the mission is the simple fact that tentmakers are in more regular and direct contact with everyday Canadians:

> It's really you're faced with that daily . . . . People watch, right; people knowing the pastor, the minister, they're watching how they respond to things, and how I treat people. And how I treat customers, and how I speak to managers. How I deal with challenges. And so, you know. It's, it's just daily life.

This kind of regular contact can offer everyday Canadians the chance to witness firsthand the transformative power of Christ at work in human lives—especially in the lives of Christian leaders. Tentmaking, by its very nature, leads to expanded missional contact surfaces and new avenues of mission. Churches often wonder how to entice our neighbors into the church building where they can be introduced to Jesus. Tentmakers have an ongoing and sustained opportunity to bring Christ to where our neighbors already are.

Tentmaking also offers the broader church more grounded insights into life in Canada. As tentmakers learn how to integrate their faith and their life at work, it can also generate new opportunities for other congregants to go and do likewise. Here is how one participant described this:

> I think the why I do what I do is because . . . ministers more generally are out of touch with what it's like to be sort of like a workaday person. And it could even put us out of touch with our own congregation where we're asking people to come to a Bible study, then a prayer meeting, then a small group, then volunteer for youth . . . and they don't appreciate what it's like to get home from a 9:00 to 5:00, eat dinner by 6:30 and then leave to go to church . . . . I think part of it is just sort of being the sort of person that I ministered to.

The Canadian church has much to gain from tentmakers. We can learn more about what it means to live out the gospel in full view of our neighbors. We can deepen our understanding of the lives, pressures, and life questions of our neighbors. We can also find new spaces in which to credibly, intelligibly, and authoritatively communicate and live out the good news about Jesus.

PART 3 | ISSUES ARISING FROM MULTIVOCATIONAL MINISTRY

Challenges

Dealing with the unique time challenges faced by tentmakers is an important consideration for denominations. Tending to the needs of tentmakers at a broader church level means developing more realistic collective expectations around time availability.

> Most denominations and movements organizations have expectations around meetings . . . all of these things, when you're bivocational, become almost impossible to attend. So, the things that are set up for either passing on information, or the things that are set up for your encouragement and strengthening whether spiritual or in ministry. All those things become an additional challenge to include in the schedule and participate in. So, there were a lot of times where I just couldn't participate in the things that the denomination had set up for my good, because generally speaking, they have organized themselves around a structure of full-time pastors who have office work through the week. Forty to fifty hours of time dedicated to serving in their church.

This is clearly a stress point and a challenge, even when intentions are good and the things that are on offer are meant to help. The unique time pressures on tentmakers means that they are not always able to participate. To make matters worse, our research did not uncover a universally open time slot or a secret new day of the week. So, for denominations that want to tend to the needs of tentmakers, they are going to need to be creative. A preliminary suggestion we could offer would be to begin designing gatherings and learning opportunities where asynchronous participation is possible. That way tentmakers can fit the opportunities into their schedule when time allows. If group cohesion depends on being together, denominations are going to need to keep tentmakers in mind as they plan.

Conclusion

By the grace of God, tentmaking will continue to be a vital ministry practice for the Canadian church both now and into the future. That being said, if this ministry practice is to be life-giving and sustainable, it must be entered into with intention and skill. Tentmakers themselves should seek out training that helps them understand and manage the unique opportunities and challenges of this mode of ministry. Local churches and local church leaders should also seek out training opportunities so that they can labor alongside tentmakers as they work to make it all possible. Finally, denominations and the broader Canadian church need to see tentmaking in a new light. Tentmaking is not a mistake. It is not a nuisance or a problem to overcome. It could very well be the key to our ongoing mission in Canada.

Questions for Reflection

1. What might be your role in helping an individual or family discern the issues they would face if they began an intentional tentmaking season of life?
2. How can congregations be helped in becoming multivocational—recognizing the multiple roles people fulfill within and outside the church?
3. What contributions do you believe the multivocational church can make to the broader church?

Bibliography

Taylor, Charles. *A Secular Age*. Cambridge, MA: Harvard University Press, 2007.
Watson, James W., et al. *Canadian Multivocational Ministry Project: Research Report*. 2020. https://www.canadianmultivocationalministry.ca/report.

Part 4

Personal Reflections from Multivocational Ministers

8

Multi-Role Ministry as a Salvation Army Officer

Michael W. Puddicombe

I APPROACH THIS CHAPTER as a practical theologian wishing to reflect on my ministry as a Salvation Army officer. Swinton and Mowat have described practical theology as a "critical, theological reflection on the practices of the church as they interact with the practices of the world, with a view of ensuring and enabling faithful participation in God's redemptive practices in, to, and for the world."[1] Theological reflection on lived contemporary experience is an important starting point for engaging practical theology. Pattison and Woodward note, "Practical theology is experiential. It takes contemporary people's experiences seriously as data for theological reflection, analysis, and thought. It also gives them high status alongside traditional authoritative texts like the bible, that contain the deposit of people's religious witness and experience in the past."[2] In describing theological reflection, Robert Kinast states, "Theological reflection is a method to help people learn from their experience. Very broadly the method of theological reflection consists of experience, reflection, and action."[3] In the case of this work, my experience as a bivocational minister, albeit a specific type of bivocational minister, will be the starting point of the theological reflection.

1. Swinton and Mowat, *Practical Theology*, 6.
2. Woodward and Pattison, "Pastoral and Practical Theology," 15.
3. Kinast, *Let Ministry Teach*, viii.

PART 4 | ISSUES ARISING FROM MULTIVOCATIONAL MINISTRY

My Situation

The early formation of my ministry started in 1990 when I took on the role of youth pastor for a Salvation Army church. I served as youth pastor for two different congregations before starting my two-year training to become a Salvation Army officer in 1995. Since our ordination (my wife and I are both ordained) in 1997, we have served in the following locations: Yellowknife, North West Territories; St. Albert, Alberta; Niagara Falls, Ontario; Thunder Bay, Ontario; Orangeville, Ontario; and we are currently serving as pastors in Burlington, Ontario. During this time, I completed my MA and PhD graduate degrees.

Until now, I have not taken the opportunity to critically reflect on my multivocational experience as a minister in The Salvation Army. As I contemplated in preparation for this critical reflection, I asked myself the following questions:

1. What is multivocational ministry?
2. How is multivocational ministry different in The Salvation Army?
3. What is my theological perspective on multivocational ministry?

As I explored these questions, I concluded that my thirty years of ministry provide a viable context for exploring multivocational ministry both in general and academically.

What Is Multivocational Ministry?

There does not seem to be a single name used to label this approach to ministry. Several terms have been used and applied in different contexts, such as "multivocational ministers," "tentmaking pastors," "bivocational leaders," "voluntary clergy," "honorary ministers," "dual-role pastors," "self-supporting pastors," and so on. Regardless of the names used to label multivocational ministers, the description used to define "multivocational" is consistent: ministers having more than one vocation. It is more common to find bivocationality in the pastoral literature with the simple definition of the roles: "one [role] that is ministry oriented and another that is outside the church."[4] This description adequately describes most bivocational

---

4. Dorsett, *Developing Leadership Teams*, 1.

situations irrespective of how the time is divided or how the ministers are remunerated.

This concept is, of course, not new to the Christian church—the prime examples being Jesus the carpenter, the fishermen apostles, and Paul the tentmaker. Although there are limited biblical references to support the view that disciples had dual roles of fishing and ministry during the time they ministered with Jesus or after his ascension, Paul's tentmaking is well documented.[5] The reality of a fully funded pastor was an anomaly in the early church, according to David Gustafson. Gustafson writes:

> Examples of bivocational ministry in the early church are common. Spyridon of Cyrus (ca. 270–348) served as bishop of Trimythous and as a shepherd. Basil of Cappadocia (330–379) reported that his priests were working and earning their daily bread. Chrysostom (ca. 347–407) spoke of rural pastors as yoking the oxen and driving the plow. Zeno (d. ca. 400), bishop of Maïouma, whose church in Gaza was quite large, was a linen weaver.[6]

From the first century to the twenty-first century, the church has always had a need for this form of ministry arrangement.

Multi-Role Experience in The Salvation Army

My experience and the experience of most Salvation Army officers regarding multivocational ministry is different from the typical definitions. It is different because we receive a salary as full-time ministers within the church, but we are given duties that extend outside the congregational ministry as well. It is not uncommon for a Salvation Army officer to be appointed to lead a congregation in a particular community and be appointed as an executive director of a social-ministry unit and/or a thrift store within that same community or a community in close proximity to the church. If the community the officer is appointed to is outside a major city, then the officer also assumes responsibility of being the public relations person for the organization. So, there are times a Salvation Army officer can wear two, three, or even four different hats as they minister within a community.

In my personal experience as a Salvation Army officer, I have had multiple roles during my entire career. For the last five years, my wife and

---

5. Watson and Santos, "Tentmaking."
6. Gustafson, "Church History of Bivo," 9.

I were responsible for a congregation, a Community and Family Services, a thrift store, and public relations and fundraising in a community. Our current appointment includes a congregation and a large Community and Family Services operation. Outside of our official responsibilities, I am also a consultant for Salvation Army congregations that are interested in undergoing a revitalization process in their church, and my wife is the chairperson for The Salvation Army Canada and Bermuda's Territorial Moral and Social Issues Committee.

Like any multivocational pastor, my time is always split between my various jobs. To devote extra time in one job means that the other job's success can suffer. My heart and my gifts are in church ministry. I enjoy preaching and teaching and making disciples and thinking of new and innovative ideas to accomplish the mission of the church. However, the missional nature of our community work cannot be neglected. Because it has been understood that The Salvation Army is the leading nongovernmental provider of social services in Canada, the work we do in the community on a daily basis and in times of emergency is important and depended upon by the community and government. So, while I would like to spend more time focusing on church work, I must be cognizant of the time necessary to foster community relationships and partnerships.

I am also responsible for raising the necessary funds for our community work. The congregants are responsible for maintaining the financial viability of the church, but community donations ensure the successful operation of our social ministries. In my current ministry appointment, our social ministries require several hundreds of thousands of dollars every year.

There have been times in my career when I have also had to oversee the operation of a thrift store. This requires a certain amount of business acumen to ensure a profitable enterprise; the profits can be used to enhance missional opportunities in the community in addition to the benefits of recycling used clothing and goods. To be sure, a thrift store that does not turn a profit is a significant stressor in the life of a Salvation Army officer, because not only do you have less funds for programs but the shortfall has to be covered through the church funds that are at times stretched thin. To be sure, over the years I have had amazing staff who have helped with all aspects of the ministry in church and social services; but in the end, the officer is responsible for the overall success or failure of the ministry.

Advantages of Multivocational Ministry

Despite—and even because of—the challenges multivocational ministry presents, it also offers some real benefits to me as the pastor and to the church. First is the missional focus it provides. By its very nature, multivocational work is missional, because the pastor is concentrating part of their time with people and situations outside of the church. Engaging in ministry that does not occur within the confines of the church building allows the pastor to be involved in the community. It is also a vehicle that allows the pastor to model to others how to be missionally minded in the workplace and community. For me, this has provided a way to solicit volunteers from the church to participate in missional ministry through a program associated with the church.

Secondly, multivocational ministry exposes the pastor to unchurched people. A pastor's time can easily be consumed by church people and church problems. By meeting regularly with those outside of the church, the pastor has an opportunity to gain an understanding of their perceptions, needs, and concerns. This has enhanced the way I communicate by ensuring that what I say is relevant to the community. My Sunday messages speak to where people are at and answer questions that they are asking.

A third benefit is leadership development. While a pastor may be the leader at the church, in their other job they may be a subordinate or partner, as part of a team. The multiple roles I must assume as a Salvation Army officer have made me a better leader. There are certain competencies required to be a leader of a church, but to lead multiple ministries at the same time demands a greater degree of capacity. For example, I am not naturally drawn to administrative tasks, so I have had to learn and hone my organizational skills, time management, volunteer coordination, and proficiency in a multitude of systems used by The Salvation Army to make my ministry fruitful.

Disadvantages to Multivocational Ministry

Without a doubt, the key disadvantage to multivocational ministry is that the church can suffer. With so many duties and only so much time, my church can often get second best. To be painfully honest, securing the monetary resources necessary to keep community programs running sometimes overshadows the ministry to the congregation. A great deal of time and energy is spent making sure the Community and Family Services programs are running efficiently, because the success of these programs helps to secure future funding. This can lead to inadequate time being spent on sermon preparation, discipleship, and pastoral-care duties—ultimately resulting in some adverse effects on the church.

The second disadvantage is the possibility of getting overwhelmed with administration minutia. This has the potential to cancel out all the advantages of multivocational ministry that I just mentioned. Reports, forms, statistics, budgets, and a multitude of other administrative tasks can overtake my time faster than anything else. If I spend most of my time adhering to the administrative responsibilities required by the denomination and government agencies, then I have less time to get from behind my desk to engage with people, be involved in missional initiatives, and effectively hone my leadership skills.

The third disadvantage is the toll that multivocational ministry can have on the family. There is a constant tug-of-war between work life and homelife, and often work wins the battle. My wife and I saw this threat to our family early in our ministry. To make sure that our family won the battle for time, we started scheduling our family time first and work responsibilities second. This gave us the chance to see all our children's concerts, school assemblies, and sports. We did not want our children growing up resenting the church because of the time lost being a family. I believe we accomplished that goal.

Theological Arguments on Multivocational Ministry in The Salvation Army Context

The Salvation Army's holistic mission ethos has been articulated as follows: "Save souls, grow saints, and serve suffering humanity." James Pedlar notes, "These three aspects of Christian mission are integrally connected in Salvationist thinking. Evangelization is intended to lead to holy living, and both evangelization and holy living require the embodied demonstration of the Gospel in service to the most vulnerable."[7] The early Salvation Army did not engage in social ministry on a large scale because they believed the conversion of sinners as being of prime importance. The dual mission of "personal salvation" and "social salvation" was firmly established in 1890 when William Booth penned these words: "Why all this apparatus of temples and

---

7. Pedlar, "O Boundless Salvation," 29.

meeting houses to save men from perdition in a world which is to come, while never a helping hand is stretched out to save them from the inferno of their present life?"[8] Booth understood that salvation was not limited to the individual but also included "social salvation from the evil that best[s] people in this life."[9] Booth did not see the social ministry of the Army as an end unto itself; rather, "the work of social redemption was preparatory, necessarily, to the work of spiritual or personal redemption."[10]

Newbigin's words illustrate this as well when he states that the gospel is "good news about God's universal reign. It is directed to the whole of human and cosmic reality."[11] He goes on to say that the perspective of the Bible indicates just such an overtone—bringing all of history and the cosmos under God's redemptive purposes.[12] It is argued, of course, that one day God will destroy the earth and create a new heaven and earth; therefore, the need to make this world a better place is counterproductive. Bosch argues that our eschatology, under the missional paradigm, must allow for tension between our participation and God's final consummation of the world. He claims, "We live between the times, between Christ's first and second coming; this is the time of the Spirit, which means that it is a time for mission. As a matter of fact, mission is the most important characteristic of and activity during this interim period. It fills the present and keeps the walls of history apart."[13] This broad view of salvation means that all the daily experiences of humanity are charged with God's presence. The flow of the Spirit can be detected and tentatively uncovered in our encounters with people.

Missio Dei and Multivocational Ministry

Mission has often been seen through the lens of personal salvation and church expansion, which tend to place our efforts at the center. Since the mid-twentieth century, there has been a shift toward understanding mission as being God's mission. Today, we see mission as an extension of God's very being. Bosch writes:

8. Booth, *In Darkest England*, 16.
9. Green, "Permanent Mission," 50.
10. Green, "Permanent Mission," 52.
11. Newbigin, *Open Secret*, 78.
12. Newbigin, *Open Secret*, 78.
13. Bosch, *Transforming Mission*, 515.

PART 4 | ISSUES ARISING FROM MULTIVOCATIONAL MINISTRY

Since God's concern is for the entire world, this should also be the scope of the *missio Dei*. It affects all people in all aspects of their existence. Mission is God's turning to the world in respect of creation, care, redemption, and consummation. It takes place in ordinary human history, not exclusively in and through the church. God's own mission is larger than the mission of the church. The *missio Dei* is God's activity, which embraces both the church and the world, and in which the church may be privileged to participate.[14]

Conclusion

Moving from practice to theory, we now return to practice. Theological reflection needs to lead to real action and real change in a real world. It is not good enough for the theological proposals to remain theoretical. The multi-role ministry of Salvation Army officers, while unique, is not dissimilar to the multivocational ministry of pastors in other denominations. We all have multiple roles to play in the church and in the community. We all experience the advantages and the disadvantages associated with being multivocational ministers. We all risk the possibility of burnout.

My personal reflection on my multivocational ministry has revealed to me the need for a theological rationale for the multi-role aspect of my ministry. Why do I do the things that I do as a Salvation Army officer? Is it because it is expected of me? Is it because this is the way ministry has been traditionally done in The Salvation Army? What about the participation of the laity in the mission of the church? This reflection also highlights the impact that multivocational ministry has made for the kingdom of God. My personal experiences have shown the missional nature of mutivocational ministry with the holistic merging of church and Community and Family Services in various contexts. Finally, this reflection has also raised questions about the ecclesiological traditions of The Salvation Army and how we engage in ministry. The Salvation Army started with the sole purpose of finding lost souls and introducing them to Jesus. The addition of social holiness in 1890 was significant in changing the ethos of the movement. Today, The Salvation Army is known worldwide not because we are a church but because we are a social organization. This fact influences the division of work and resources as officers with multiple roles. Which gets

14. Bosch, *Transforming Mission*, 401.

more time and energy, the church or the social services? This reflection has shown that our ecclesiological traditions help to shape the way we do practical theology and that these traditions can evolve when we reflect on them theologically.

Questions for Reflection

1. From your perspective, what would you consider to be the benefits and challenges of fulfilling multiple roles?
2. In what ways has your ecclesiological tradition shaped your approach to ministry?
3. How has your theological reflection directed your participation in God's mission?

Bibliography

Booth, William. *In Darkest England and a Way Out.* London: Salvation Army, 1890.
Bosch, David J. *Transforming Mission: Paradigm Shifts in Theology of Mission.* 20th anniv. ed. Maryknoll, NY: Orbis, 2014.
Dorsett, T. *Developing Leadership Teams in the Bivocational Church.* Bloomington, IN: CrossBooks, 2010.
Green, Roger J. "A Permanent Mission to the 'Whosoever': William Booth's Theology of Redemption." In *Saved, Sanctified and Serving: Perspectives on Salvation Army Theology and Practice,* edited by Denis Metrustery, 42–57. Bletchley, UK: Paternoster, 2016.
Gustafson, David. "A Church History of Bivo." *EFCA Today* 91.1 (2016) 8–11. https://www.efcatoday.org/story/church-history-bivo.
Kinast, Robert L. *Let Ministry Teach: A Guide to Theological Reflection.* Collegeville, MN: Liturgical, 1996.
Newbigin, Lesslie. *The Open Secret: An Introduction to the Theology of Mission.* Grand Rapids: Eerdmans, 1995.
Pedlar, James E. "O Boundless Salvation: Save Souls, Grow Saints, and Serve Suffering Humanity—The Army's Holistic Vision." In *Saved, Sanctified and Serving: Perspectives on Salvation Army Theology and Practice,* edited by Denis Metrustery, 29–41. Bletchley, UK: Paternoster, 2016.
Swinton, John, and Harriet Mowat. *Practical Theology and Qualitative Research.* London: SCM, 2006.
Watson, James W., and Narry F. Santos. "Tentmaking: Creative Mission Opportunities within a Secularizing Canadian Society." In *Mission and Evangelism in a Secularizing World,* edited by Narry Santos and Mark Naylor, 131–48. Eugene, OR: Pickwick, 2019.

PART 4 | ISSUES ARISING FROM MULTIVOCATIONAL MINISTRY

Woodward, James, and Stephen Pattison. "An Introduction to Pastoral and Practical Theology." In *The Blackwell Reader in Pastoral and Practical Theology*, edited by James Woodward and Stephen Pattison, 1–19. Malden, MA: Blackwell, 2000.

9

Being a Professor in the City and a Pastor in the Country

James Tyler Robertson

In my living room hangs a picture of Saint Thomas Aquinas. He has a well-lined face and a mouth that is turned down, and his mournful eyes look up and to the right, reminding me of the famous line in Ecclesiastes: "With much wisdom comes much sorrow."[1] But his hands always grab my attention. In his left hand is an open book, open in such a way that the viewer can see the red and black lettering inside; in his right hand is a building—presumably a church—that is tall enough to extend from his lower torso to just above the top of his shaven head. This artistic interpretation of the famous medieval scholar provides my visual mission statement as a bivocational minister and professor.

The academy—represented by the book—finds true purpose only in service to the church. Without the right hand, the left hand would be content to remain pouring over books, concerned only with academic theories that excite the minds of intellectuals. The right hand forces the left to ask the question: How does this actually impact the lives of church people? On the other side, the church benefits from the critical thinking that the academy demands of all her children. Such thinking can combat harmful or vapid theology, move leadership beyond shifting trends, and assist the laity

---

1. "For with much wisdom comes much sorrow; the more knowledge, the more grief" (Eccl 1:18 NIV).

in their personal theological reflections. If I may be permitted to change Jesus' maxim in Matt 6:3, it is crucial in this tentmaking ministry for the left and right hands to very much know what the other is doing.[2]

When I first learned of this project, I must confess that I did not see myself as bivocational because both vocations intersect seamlessly enough to appear, on first look, like two sides of the same coin. Upon further examination, a deeper reality became apparent. Both jobs require different skill sets, have different (and sometimes competing) emphases, and have language and wisdom that cannot be found in the other. Therefore, this chapter will focus on my role as a pastor/professor who works in a Toronto-based university while also serving two small Baptist churches in the rural countryside of southwestern Ontario.

This chapter will be broken into three sections: family, rhythm, and change. The family section will speak of my origins at Westover Church and Mountsberg Baptist Church, how these communities changed my perspective on the role of pastor, and how letting go of my program ideas transformed a church community into a faith family. The rhythm section—through the lens of a church picnic—will explain the wisdom of the rural landscape and how that changed my theology of mission. Finally, I will explain how my academic expertise has provided new opportunities for lifelong Christians to change their known and loved Sunday-morning worship experience! The argument of this chapter is that my academic study and lived experiences in Westover and Mountsberg have given me a more robust definition of "church." This chapter, like the painting of Aquinas, is about finding balance between the theories of the academy and the realities of the church.

Family

Midway through my doctoral studies, I moved to the countryside of Flamborough to begin my time as the pastor of a rural two-point charge. This meant that I would be the pastor of two connected, though separate and distinct, faith communities.

Mountsberg and Westover have been connected since the times of their respective origins in the 1840s. They were teaching churches where young seminarians would "cut their teeth" on preaching, home/hospital

---

2. "But when you give to the needy, do not let your left hand know what your right hand is doing" (Matt 6:3 NIV).

visits, board meetings, and the other activities that make up church ministry. I was among the most experienced of their recent hires, as I had already worked in a variety of churches over the years and possessed a master of divinity degree. These communities are generous and gracious and possess a wisdom and patience that comes from knowing that they outlast any minister that graces their pulpit for a season. They enjoyed their ministers, were supportive of them, and basically showed young up-and-comers the ropes, all the while knowing that someday soon these people would move on to other churches.

It took me about two years to realize that these churches were not stepping-stones to something bigger or better; these churches were about the best communities one could hope to lead. And that realization came following a meeting I had with one of my denominational leaders as I struggled with personal and professional issues. As I wondered about my future, his sage advice was "Pastor them how to pastor you," and that altered the dynamics of our communities.

I have cried in front of these people so many times. They have seen me preach while struggling with my own faith. They have waited patiently while I left, mid-sermon, to go change a diaper, and they have cooked for me, called me, hugged me, and healed me. These are patient people who are used to teaching their pastors. Sure, I did not need as much advice on sermon preparation; I needed more help in my daily life. For all my Greek lessons, historical references, and biblical knowledge, I can honestly say that it was these small, red-brick churches that showed me why we call the gospel "good news" and why church attendance is so important.

My studies reduced my mental and emotional energy and made it impossible to accomplish all the big plans I had for these little communities. Like all pastors, I had dreams to make something more of these churches, and growing up in the city, that usually meant bringing busy and disparate people together to experience the communal elements that church can offer through programs and creative events. But this was not to be the case with the rural churches I was pastoring.

These are the hardest-working people I have ever met, and they learned long ago that the only way to succeed in the cold climate of Canada is through cooperation and community. They relish social time with each other, and for some, that social time requires a spiritual gravitas not present in the Optimists, Lions, Women's Institutes, or other rural social organizations. My outreach programs fell by the side because these two churches did not need instruction in community building but were hungrier to see how their faith really mattered in daily life.

Authenticity, more than events or expertise, carried the day, and their grace set me free to see the stories of salvation and redemption in my own mistakes and bring such lessons into my Sunday-morning messages—and my Monday-to-Saturday interactions with them as well. This has been a very difficult path, and I have frequently questioned my pastoral worthiness; but it also taught me that as soon as one thinks he or she is ready for ministry, that is a pretty good indication that the exact opposite is true.

Pastoring them to pastor me set me free to be a more authentic version of myself and finally understand my preaching professor's line: for all the reasons people attend church, the only question they have is this: Have you seen God, and what does God look like? As any of us who have walked with God long enough realize, we tend to see God clearer in our struggles. Those very struggles sparked my theological reflection and my communities' acceptance of my flawed humanity and led us all to shared personal growth. When people ask me how I am able to pastor two churches with all my busy academic responsibilities, I reply that I do not lead two churches, but that I belong to two families.

Rhythm

It was not until I began my rural ministry that I understood how important Jesus' carpentry was to his ministry. I also learned that a city guy teaching agricultural parables to farmers is all the wrong kinds of audacity. After one very thorough and profound message on the parable of the sower, a member of the church told me, "I liked the stuff about Jesus you just said; the farming stuff was all wrong, but the Jesus stuff was nice," and then shook my hand, clapped me on the back, and walked out of the church.[3] If ever a compliment put me in my place, that was the one!

At a Mountsberg picnic, I casually mentioned how much I wanted corn on the cob. I was greeted by a collective outburst of laughter before someone finally relieved my confused expression by informing me, "It's not corn season yet!" At another time, I was having coffee with a member of Westover, and we were talking about the weather and the work he was planning for the upcoming winter. I asked him why he was not doing such things sooner, and he simply replied, "That's what winter is for. We can't do

3. Matt 13:1–23.

much with the land, so we take care of the other stuff." It took a while for the profundity of those two stories to set in.

Growing up in the city, I could eat what I want, pretty much when I want it. But farmers know the rhythm of crops, the rhythm of life. For most of my life—and due in no small part to my discipline as a historian—time has been a linear construct. A linear construct with little predictability, a collection of experiences and events that are related to actions and consequences but also have unbelievable ability to surprise and shock. Much of my counseling and teachings on the importance of faith have come from reminding people that the tragedies of life are rarely predictable and can strike quite easily on a sunny Tuesday afternoon.

Historiography itself teaches that many have studied the past in order to detect patterns in human movements to see if predicting the future is possible from a scientific standpoint. Despite those who claim to have discovered that the world repeats itself every several centuries or so, as far as I can tell, "those who cannot remember the past are condemned to repeat it" is as close as we can come to offering insight into what is yet to be.[4] That has helped my academic pursuits, as historians never attempt to predict the future.

However, I have struggled to use this perspective in helpful ways in ministry, especially when genuine tragedy occurs. Sitting in the kitchen of a woman whose son was recently murdered stands out as a time when my understanding of life seemed inadequate to the task before me. That unbelievably heavy moment, paired to the comical corn incident and fairly innocuous conversation about winter chores offered new insight and, interestingly enough, practical applications that my theories failed to do.

Eating food that is in season and saving certain jobs for certain times of year taught me that the rhythm of life is seasonal, not strictly linear. If suffering is winter, then the person should be set free to feel all the feelings that come with winter; knowing all the while that spring is coming, even if we don't know exactly when. After the senseless death of a child, agony descends as unbidden and unavoidable as the winter season. Loneliness, cold, darkness, and the inability to handle previous tasks define this season of life, as ominous and never-ending as that season can appear. Rhythm

---

4. Although there is debate, this saying is most frequently attributed to George Santayana. Nicholas Clairmont, "'Those Who Do Not Learn History Are Doomed to Repeat It.' Really?," Big Think, July 31, 2013, https://bigthink.com/culture-religion/those-who-do-not-learn-history-doomed-to-repeat-it-really/.

offers a quiet reminder that spring will eventually arrive, just as stubbornly as the winter.

Thus, the sorrowful kitchen became a conversation about embracing the activities and thoughts that can only be done in a season of mourning. Heartache was embraced, and loneliness and anger became a facet of everyday life, just like the snows of winter—sometimes so forceful that one could only see or hear the storm. At other times, the sadness was calmer but nevertheless all around, just like the snow remains on the ground and in the bare tree branches on even the sunniest of winter days.

The rhythm of grief does, somewhat counterintuitively, lead to healing and joy, an internal spring in which we begin to see the point of reexperiencing life. Spring leads into the joy and sunshine of summer, a season of other activities. Then comes the inevitable pull of autumn that yields more crops, a season of hard work in which we reflect and gain wisdom and insight provided by the activities of the other seasons.

Thus, in the words of Ecclesiastes again, everything has its season, and there is a time for everything under heaven.[5] A rhythmic understanding combats the trite, because it does not pat the grief-stricken on the back and push them toward feeling better. It does not hurry through Good Friday or Holy Saturday but sees necessity in that despair—a beautiful despair that makes Easter Sunday so much better. As strange as this may sound, not being able to eat corn in June taught me how to sit with people who experience loss or terror and see the power in their personal winter. It grants me permission to sit in silent sadness, knowing that words can no more move a person toward healing than my longing for warmer days can shorten winter. It gives the grieved permission to simply sit in the sadness and reject the pressure to get better or do something. These patient people, attuned to the rhythm of our world and dependent on the attitude of the earth for their living, showed me the patience and humility that must come to all of us living in this beautiful, fractured, seasonal world.

This "earth wisdom" showed me why Jesus pointed to seeds, birds, gusts of wind, or patches of dirt to show people the deep truths of the cosmos. It helped me see the redemptive power of the incarnation, because despite the teachings of many believers throughout history, this world is not doomed or damned or dirty but is the displayer of God's salvation for those who have eyes to see and ears to hear. Honestly, it has kept me from buying corn on the cob in January because I know that it is a food out of

5. Eccl 3:1–8.

season. While immediately gratifying, eating out of season robs me of the chance to experience the rhythm of life established by God. In other words, corn is a sermon to me now.

Change

I do not want to create the impression that my rural pastorate is all sunshine and wonders of earthy wisdom; my other job as professor has helped my faith families grow as well. The more I study the history of the Christian faith, the more I begin to realize that deep movements are not about numbers or influence but about small collections of people genuinely following their faith.

One summer, we began to forego the traditional sermon time and moved our services into the basement of Mountsberg and the backroom of Westover. We would still gather to sing and pray, but the latter half of the service was dedicated to conversations related to matters of faith. Since it was summer (when new ideas can be more easily embraced), people enjoyed the novelty of it all.

At first, we left it wide open, but that sometimes brought us into tangents and inconsequential conversations. In the end, we discovered a productive blend of brief reflection from me, followed up by a time of discussion about a topic of faith. We talked openly about the struggles of aging. We spent four weeks discussing whether or not church actually matters or if faith can grow outside the structures of religion. We challenged and discussed the notion that Jesus is the only way to heaven. By the end of the summer, most people wanted to maintain that rhythm, and that is what we have been doing for over half a decade now.

This has really challenged people, and some have left because of it. Pushing back against my elders on beliefs that I think are more cultural than biblical has created some tense moments but also some real vulnerability and growth. I truly believe these moments have only been possible because our churches are small and because everyone knows each other really well.

This is where my ability to think on my feet and lean heavily on my studies has served my people well. I can go into a Sunday morning confident that I have years of education and teaching experience from which to draw. I know how ideas and people have shaped Christianity; that allows these people, many of whom have been faithful for over seven decades, to see their Jesus in new ways. I spend less time in my study reading books for Sunday and more time getting to listen to the collective faith present around the table each week. Members of our little churches openly share with each other where each of us has seen God during the week, and we have only grown deeper and closer because of that. Not to mention that the unbelievable gift of being a pastor who gets to glean wisdom from his family weekly has corrected a trend that dominated the early years of my ministry.

I worked with the young and, like most, know that the church is in numerical decline and, without young people, is destined to simply die. However, the rich experiences and lives present in these little churches makes the idea of courting the young seem like folly to me. For all my rhetorical ecclesiology, I truly wanted a cool church that other people talked about, but now I want only to continue growing with my little faith families. We have no budget for marketing, no website (which is even funnier given that I am the director of online learning at the university), one church sign that is on its last legs, another church whose sign is perpetually behind a giant shrub, and no community programs. Ours is a church dedicated to staying small, growing deep, and welcoming anyone God brings to our doors; and God has brought a surprising collection of people.

That is where my scholarship has helped, because I am hoping to set my people free from the pressure to "go back to the glory days" by reminding them that the ebbs and flows they taught me about crops also apply to their sacred little communities. Something has not gone wrong; the church in Canada is just in a different season, and this season has chores of its own. My study of history has provided stories and people that have shaped the world for the past two thousand years, and I get to remind my faith families that such a legacy means Westover and Mountsberg will exist for as long as God needs them and not one second more or less.

Conclusion

What does the future hold for these small communities in underpopulated sections of Canada? Well, thanks to my role as a professor, I have colleagues and friends who do research into this and provide me with tremendous sociological, theological, ecclesiological, and pastoral resources few other pastors can claim. I know the importance of real-estate data as well as medieval theologians and twenty-first-century farming techniques. These churches are bucking the trend by remaining small and simply doing things that amuse them (like annual variety shows, pig roasts, and collecting scrap metal from farmers), and somehow both have some legs to remain on the landscape of Canada for quite some time.

I am grateful for the opportunity to reflect upon my time at Mountsberg and Westover as a professor and how these two facets of my life, while complementary, have very different appeals to me. I cannot help but joke about board meetings when I teach on wars in Christian history, and I cannot help but bring in ideas (and occasionally students) from the classroom to see what my Sunday people think. Both students and parishioners benefit from the practical advice and experience of an academic pastor. Both students and parishioners, in some beautiful instances, have been set free from ideas that had been harming them.

My propensity is to think that church life keeps me honest and grounded and informs my teaching more than the other way around. However, my decade of ministry in the country has shown me the power of language and the need for Christians, no matter what kind of church they attend, to be a thinking people. I would not have learned about the rhythms of life or the power of community without my little faith families, but nor would I have the capacity to reflect on and speak about the deep spirituality that underpins such things if I were not a professor. And so, I return to the image of Aquinas that hangs in my cozy country room surrounded by my own books and trappings of the academy. I am pleased, because it seems that when it comes to bivocational ministry, my life appears to be imitating that art.

Questions for Reflection

1. Can/should a pastor challenge his/her congregation to change—or even jettison—church traditions that he/she believes are holding the church back? What if these traditions are respected and perhaps crucial to that church's identity?
2. How important do you think higher education is for pastors?
3. Do you think pastors should be able to open up from the pulpit about their personal doubts?

10

Twenty-Eight Years and Counting

CAM ROXBURGH

How could I continue to plant this church and start up a sports ministry at the same time? The elders wrestled with the question, and I got the answer I wanted; however, I began to realize that the original question had been naive and theologically shallow. The question should not have been "*How* could I do this?" but rather "*Why* would I do this?" Twenty-seven years later, I have learned that even the "why" question needed more reflection. Why be a tentmaker? Why should a leader of a church be bivocational or covocational (as some prefer to call it)? What if we pushed even one step deeper and asked, "Why are we even asking the why question?" Although, in this chapter, I will tell my story of being a tentmaker for twenty-eight years, describing the pitfalls and the benefits of such a life, I want to address not just the answers to the question "Why tentmaker?" but also the theological and practical underpinnings behind the question.

My Story

Only six months after accepting the role of being a church planter with the Canadian Baptists of Western Canada (CBWC), I was offered the opportunity to start the Athletes in Action soccer ministry—a role I had dreamed about most of my life. I could not possibly quit on the church plant after such a short time, could I? The CBWC had invited me to become a tentmaker by moving into the manse and getting another job locally. As a recent graduate with bills, only a few years of marriage under my belt, a year-old daughter, and another on the way, I had a strong opinion about this. I suggested that they sell me the manse and take the money and put it back into paying my salary. This would also allow us money to renovate the church building and to bank the other half for a future church plant. They agreed, and my journey into becoming a bivocational pastor was delayed. I began in the summer of 1992, but by the spring of 1993, the opportunity of the sports ministry had come. I would do both for three years and then step aside from the church. I liked to start things. I was also not satisfied with doing just one thing. Having my finger in different pies allowed me to keep the boredom of routine at bay. This was not a sign of strength but more likely of immaturity; however, it was a contributing factor in my journey of being what we call "bivocational."

For the last twenty-eight years, I have always had two or more jobs, and I do not regret it. Southside grew and multiplied. After three years, I stepped aside from the Athletes in Action leadership, as I had fallen in love with the church. God was clearly at work. I had opportunities to tell our ministry story, and before long, Church Planting Canada invited me to lead their growing movement. I was immediately drawn to their team and vision and felt that I had something to offer, thinking through not just how many churches we could plant but, more importantly, what kind of churches were needed in the now post-Christian context that we found ourselves in. My time was now given to the church and leading a church-planting organization. Young and vibrant leaders (as if I were old at thirty-two) had been drawn to Southside and were hungry for training. It was our conviction to train new leaders in the church rather than to send them off to seminary alone. The theological work at seminary was important, but not without the very intentional work of leadership training in a local neighborhood. The Missional Training Network was developed and began to take more and more of my time. This ministry is now known as Forge Canada, which has helped to shape leaders, churches, and even denominations in missional theology and ecclesiology across the country. One denomination, The North American Baptists (NAB), was so particularly impacted that it invited me to serve with their international office as vice president (VP) of missional initiatives. Although the offer was for a full-time role, I was convinced of the importance of leading locally while I trained others.

Today, I lead Southside, serve as VP in the NAB, and lead Forge globally. Is there such a thing as trivocational? I often come across wonderful

PART 4 | ISSUES ARISING FROM MULTIVOCATIONAL MINISTRY

leaders who serve mutivocationally out of necessity. I respect them for their love of the church. Others serve bivocationally as a strategy to keep "one foot in the world." Staff members at Southside have multiple jobs because we embody the conviction that we are part of a community of God's people who have been sent into neighborhoods to join God on mission. We do not merely have jobs at the church; instead, we are gifts to the church to help it to be faithful in following Christ on mission. We each have other jobs in the neighborhood for kingdom growth. It is a strategy for being involved, a means of supporting the church, and a deep theological conviction. At times, the church supports us financially so as to free us to give more time to leading as needed.

The Pitfalls

The journey is not always easy. There are pitfalls that need to be noted. The first, most obvious pitfall is overwork. There is a never-ending amount of work in church leadership. Many in ministry have a high need to help others and to provide solutions in the midst of crisis. This combination makes overwork a real issue. Add another job into the mix, and it becomes like turbocharging an already-fast car. Along with overwork, other pitfalls include lack of sleep, overeating, increased pace of life, and personality changes. At the top of this impressive heap, decay of your own soul is often a reality. Dallas Willard made a clear statement about most pastors in one of my classes. Pastors lack sleep and live at such a pace that they are unable to listen to the voice of God, even if they are trying. With much clatter in their lives, they are unable to discern his voice.

A second pitfall is the lack of a clear "first thing." I am asked, "Which role/job do I wake up thinking about?" If one of your jobs is working at Starbucks, then perhaps it is easier to keep the church as the top priority. But if you get promoted to store manager and have to deal with a crisis—like how to stay profitable during a pandemic, this may well change. Bob Biehl, in an Arrow Leadership seminar I attended, stated that in order to lead well, you must give 90 percent of your energy and focus to the one thing. In working two jobs, there is a danger that the church is not the first thing, and your focus on helping the church be faithful may suffer. A third pitfall follows: modeling the wrong thing can be true of multivocational leaders. I am convinced that the best way to lead is through modeling the life of Christ and not just with words. I have had to ask if my pace and focus on "first things" have modeled how Christ actually lived. I once was told that people love to follow me because of vision, but there are few who want to imitate my life. Multivocational leaders must constantly be asking the questions of motives and of character formation in themselves. Are they wholly ambitious or do they have holy intentions?

A fourth pitfall is that it is easy to demonstrate a lack of love for the people of the church. If overworked and the pace of life has escalated, the danger is that you may feel frustrated and display a lack of love. Others often sense it in you long before you realize it about yourself. The gift you have been to the church and the reason you entered into ministry in the first place are replaced with a "getting the job done" mentality that lacks the kind of patience and caring needed to lead the community well. King Saul is one example in Scripture of this pitfall.

A final pitfall (do we need more?) is that these all work together to cause people to view you through a different set of lenses. My involvement with other things, the pace of life, and the long work hours have drawn respect from many of the people, but they also see me as unavailable and unapproachable. It is not that I am not loved; it is just that I can be excluded from the "fun things of life" that are not "official business." This has created the pain of loneliness. It is part of leadership, but it can become even greater in the midst of multivocationalism.

Benefits

With all of those pitfalls, it would seem as if I were steering you away from multivocational ministry, but I am wanting to convince you that there are many benefits. We have misunderstood the difference between a job and a vocation. My theological conviction is that although we may have any number of jobs, Christ followers have but one vocation. They are called to serve as local missionaries in a local community of God's people. Although God's people have gifts, they also "are" gifts to the local church community. It has been my privilege to have been called as a missionary of Christ, belonging to a local church called Southside and using my gifts and passions to help lead them where God has called us. I have had a number of jobs but have been grateful that the church has seen the need to free up some of my time to lead well and contribute to the well-being of my family. Therefore, I am not sure I like the word "multivocational."

PART 4 | ISSUES ARISING FROM MULTIVOCATIONAL MINISTRY

Perhaps we might simply say we have multiple jobs or income streams. There are many personal and corporate benefits to having multiple income streams. The first benefit is that it helps leaders to be normal. What do I mean by "normal"? For too long, the church has produced a system where "pastors" have been seen as a different breed—like goalies in hockey. We have placed them on a pedestal, spiritually above others. Much is to be expected of leaders, but I am not convinced it means we become a different breed. Our neighbors need to see that we are like them. I have enjoyed that kind of reputation with my neighbors for all these years. Being normal allows me to be creative with answering the question of what I do for a job. I am not embarrassed to call myself a "pastor," but I must read the situation and determine which answer will be best received. Calling myself a "neighborhood transformation consultant"—teaching people how to be better neighbors and transform neighborhoods—is often well received and has opened many conversational doors. Being normal has also paid dividends in preaching and teaching opportunities. The church knows that I am constantly rubbing shoulders with other normal people and that I have a grasp on what they are going through. My words have a greater chance of landing.

A second benefit is the contribution it makes to the dismantling of the clergy–laity divide. I want our people to see me as normal and to see themselves as full-time missionaries. We must get away from the idea that leaders are "paid to do that" and move toward a theological understanding and practice that leaders are there for equipping others to be participants and not just spectators. Staff having multiple jobs is part of living out this theological conviction.

A third benefit is that it allows us to model the life of a follower of Jesus. People today want to see the difference that Christ makes in your life and not just to hear about it. Having spoken of the pitfalls, we also want to demonstrate the life of a disciple. If we pay attention to how I live this out, the why will become evident. We model such things as work ethic and work relationships. We model leadership and discipline. We model the way in which a leader submits to the community and to the use of gifts in supporting the community. From the beginning of my own journey with Southside Community Church, we have leaned into the idea of multivocationalism not because we did not have enough money but because we believed deeply in leadership modeling—what it looks like to not just speak of the way we should follow Jesus in the world but to live it.

A fourth benefit has to do with freeing up of resources to put toward other staff and other ministries. This helps us to break away from a Christendom model of a jack-of-all-trades pastor on whom the church becomes dependent. The church recognizes a variety of giftings in others and can support those who need it. It is a fundamentally different picture of how the church should be structured and function. It reflects a New Testament church structure, where people are not paid to do the role of leadership but rather receive funding as the church needs them to have more time for equipping. It pushes us away from *pastoring as a job* toward leading by offering ourselves as a gift. It encourages us to earn money in other areas so that we, too, can contribute to the funding of the mission that we are joining God on. Every year, I take a group of fifty or so leaders to Chicago to spend three days with David Fitch. Gathering at his church, David shares the story of who they are and to what they believe God has called them. Along with them, we see the value of freeing up resources to allow others to join the team and to use this money to support others in the neighborhood.

Permit me to add just one other benefit. At one level, it is a personal benefit, but perhaps it cannot be separated from also being a benefit to the whole community. Having multiple sources of income has cost my family and me, but it has also opened some very exciting doors. I have remained on the front edge of belonging to a community of God's people who are not satisfied with "We have always done it that way" but rather are seeking to join with God in what he is currently doing. It has forced us to constantly re-envision how we do things based on the why. We are constantly looking toward God's future.

The Church of the Future

These are strange times, but perhaps not a lot different from some past periods of church history. COVID-19 has been a mirror for the church—exposing things that get in the way of us joining God on mission. It has also served as an accelerant to the church—pushing us more quickly toward a future that many saw as inevitable. Secularism is forcing the church to change the way that we see ourselves and function. No longer do we hold a place of privilege at the center of our culture. Tax benefits and perhaps charitable status have long been rumored to be on their way out in Canada. Charitable-giving receipts are a help and allow the church to continue to operate with larger staff. But what happens if, in the near future, the benefits are reduced and the costs continue to go up? What happens when the cost of living in places like Vancouver and Toronto gets so high that churches are unable to pay the necessary pastors' salaries needed to support a family in their neighborhood? What happens when the cost of purchasing a property or renting a facility becomes too high? What happens when we are not allowed to rent facilities like schools as we once were?

We are being forced to imagine a new way of being the church, and this is a good thing. We are in many ways seeing an end to the Christendom model of doing church and being invited into being God's people who join him on mission. Stepping into a new way of leading may start with a fresh vision of how we live, are paid, and spend our time. Instead of hiring pastors to spend the bulk of their time preparing to preach, we need leaders who equip us to correctly handle God's truth in Scripture. Instead of relying on a certain person to do all the evangelism, we have been invited to foster a passion for being and sharing the good news among all of God's people. Instead of paying someone to put on a service where we shop for our religious goods and services, we have been forced into discovering the beauty of becoming a people who find their identity as part of the family of God and joining him on mission in the neighborhood. Instead of putting all of our finances into the sustaining of a staff who put on programs, we free up funds to serve the needs of the neighborhood to which we have been sent. Instead of . . . well, I am sure there will be more. For sure, there are costs to the idea of multivocationalism, but they do not even come close to the benefits that are received. And even if there were less benefits, I am convinced of both the theological correctness of this road we are on and the practical importance to the church that God is desiring for the future of our land. The future of God's people is bright and perhaps not as alarming as we may think.

Questions for Reflection

1. Which pitfall concerns you the most? Why does it bother you? How could you avoid it?
2. How would you list the benefits of tentmaking? Which do you feel are most significant? Why?
3. Where can you recognize opportunities for living missionally in your situation?

11

Ministry or Career?
An Unnecessary Dichotomy

AMY BRATTON AND ASHOOR YOUSIF

"You need to meet Dr. Ashoor Yousif. He has a great story of multivocational ministry and is very insightful in how he understands his story." That's how Dr. James Watson first approached me about working on a chapter for this book about tentmaking ministry in Canada. I have to admit, I was curious. I met with Dr. Yousif via videoconference from where I sat in Saskatoon, and he joined me from Mississauga. His story and his insights did not disappoint. What we offer in this chapter is a collaboration between me (Amy Bratton) and Dr. Ashoor Yousif to take a look at his experience of multivocational ministry as part of a team ministry—where he illustrates that the choice between ministry or career is an unnecessary dichotomy.

We introduced ourselves, and then Ashoor shared with me that he came to faith in the church where he is now a pastor when he migrated to Canada as a young person. As he grew in faith, Middle Eastern Baptist Church (MEBC) gave him opportunities to serve. As he studied and completed an engineering degree, he continued to volunteer his time at the church, and at this same time, the church was also growing and changing as their ministry developed.

This congregation provides a worship context in Arabic for a variety of people of different nationalities from the Middle East. This worshiping community was gathered by a group of lay leaders and employed pastors who were themselves first-generation immigrants to Canada. As the years passed and MEBC continued to develop its own character, it became harder to find a leader from outside the worshiping community who was a good fit for the congregation. While continuing to find connection to each other through worship in Arabic, the congregation was also being shaped by its particular location in Canada.

Balancing this tension between cultures can happen in any church with various subcultures, yet congregations who worship together in a language other than Canada's official languages of English and French are faced with the tension between the Canadian culture and the culture of the language in which they worship. Tension can be resolved in favor of one side or the other. Or tension can be leveraged to create something beautiful.

Many of the research participants from the Canadian Multivocational Ministry Project described the uniqueness of their ministry situation.[1] It is somewhat ironic that the commonality of the multivocational ministers was their uniqueness. Many of these ministers with unique callings were obviously richer for having engaged in the wider community through their work or for having expressed another side of their personality, making space to create something beautiful where there might have been a troublesome tension. Finding a healthy way to live in tension produced positive results.

Getting back to Ashoor's story, as his congregation felt the tension that was creating a unique culture within MEBC, the leadership moved toward a new way of organizing pastoral ministry. Rather than seek out another leader from outside the church, they shifted to a team approach and started looking at how the congregation's members were developed into leaders from within the context of MEBC. Not only was there the team of pastors, but in each area of ministry there was a team of volunteers that worked together to lead the ministries of the church. As the parishioners saw this pattern modeled by their multivocational pastors, a path toward involvement was opened up for teams of people to contribute together.

As this shift in perspective was taking place, Ashoor had been ministering to his peers and was being mentored. While working as a biomedical electrical engineer, he also sought out theological training through the MTS Modular program that focused on those who were currently working while completing their studies at Tyndale Seminary. On completion of his graduate degree, in Ashoor's words, "the church recognized one of its sons

---

1. Watson et al., *Canadian Multivocational Ministry Project*.

as qualified to lead it and called me to be part of it." Organically from within the church, Ashoor was given a leadership role among a team of multivocational ministers. He was on the team of ministers, but beyond the pastoral team, the whole church also shifted to seeing ministry as a team project with volunteers engaging in ministry together. As Ashoor shared during our conversation, "I joined an already-existing team of three pastors, and I was the fourth. They mentored me, shepherded me, and put the loads on my shoulders that fit my gifts and also my time."

As he took on leadership, he continued to work as an engineer and volunteer his time in ministry. This balancing of a multivocational life was a continuation for him, as he had balanced study and work throughout his engineering degree and his theological studies. When I asked about balancing pastoring and working as an engineer, Ashoor responded, "It had its beauty and it had its challenges." He went on to share that the beauty of working as an an engineer alongside pastoring was that it gave him insight into the life of his parishioners, breaking down the barrier between lay and clergy as they each balanced work and ministry, modeling for the people he shepherded that they, too, could do the ministry to which they felt called in the church alongside their vocational work. Ashoor shared that he was blessed by this team approach not only because he was working while pastoring but because it made space for rest and restoration. When working on a team, you always know you can take a break because you have a team that you can trust around you.

One thing that paves the way for a team approach to leadership is a theological affirmation of work. Ashoor has been formed by his theological studies, which affirmed the goodness of work and of all vocations. While the research findings of the Canadian Multivocational Ministry Project also noted the importance of multivocational ministers having a sense of calling to their ministry as a source for resiliency, Ashoor framed the call to a life of multivocational pursuits with further nuance.[2] When I asked him about his theology of work, he mentioned that he enjoys working with young people who are shaping their lives and thinking about how they will arrange work in their lives. Will they respond to the push in our culture to have a career, have a family, and have a house and will they make choices about their work based on those pursuits? And as they achieve these goals, where will they find meaning in these things? While one narrative places meaning on sacrificing these pursuits for spiritual pursuits (to become a

---

2. Watson et al., *Canadian Multivocational Ministry Project*.

missionary overseas, for example), yet it comes as a relief to many of these young people to hear that they can be *called* to the vocation that they have been pursuing. As Ashoor shared, "They find that their passion for their job could be enhanced by their love for God. If they do it out of a passion and love for God, then they are going to do a better job and they are going to do a job that will satisfy God." Furthermore, he noted:

> The last thing you want is for people to live with the idea that only a few are called by God to serve him, not everybody is called. Because what happens, especially among young people who are establishing their lives, and sometimes among older people who have been in the faith for a while, is that there are these silos of life—church, family, work—and they don't see the integration of all of them together in God's designs or plan.

Thinking in silos can lead to assumptions about what aspects of life one can seek God's will in. Do we seek God's guidance on our vocation if it is not a ministry vocation? Do we isolate aspects of our life as we seek God's guidance, keeping parts of our life in those silos? Or do we instead bring our whole life before God?

> When we are praying in any one of those items [of life] we're praying out of an understanding of the whole calling that God has called us to, and the different aspects of what God has been doing in our life and continues to do.... I know it is difficult to bring the overall picture of how God sees into our head, but we should seek to see how the story of our life is unfolding when God is intervening and he keeps trying to bring all these things together.[3]

This thinking shaped how Ashoor approached his own discernment regarding the shift. After completing his master's degree in theological studies, he was serving as a pastor and continuing his work as an engineer but also felt a call toward further theological studies. As he prayed and discerned, he examined his gifts and calling, and he moved toward the academic world while also feeling a call to continue in pastoral ministry. As he pursued his PhD, there was an intentional multivocational plan to continue in his pastoral role. There has been synergy between his PhD studies and now his teaching role at Tyndale alongside his pastoral work. He can bring his academic studies into the congregation to enrich their life together. He

---

3. Ashoor's words.

is a practitioner bringing his pastoral experience to his students at Tyndale who are training for ministry.

So, in light of this nuanced understanding of calling, which includes the call of God on all aspects of life, it was not a surprise that Ashoor also had wise words to share about the pressures of living a multivocational life. When someone is called to multivocational ministry, not taking on other employment because of financial pressures, lack of opportunities, or other limitations but living a calling to multivocational ministry, then the pressures that come with multivocational ministry can be faced with more confidence. There are specific pressures that come with this type of life, such as the struggle to enjoy the moment and keep life balanced. In addition, he noted:

> You may need to accept that the multivocational call is about succeeding to a certain level in multiple tasks, rather than excelling in one, because that is not your calling. Then you will drop this internal sense of guilt or the competitive spirit with why this neighboring church or colleague is that successful because that's all they do, they are on staff. You will know that there are benefits and consequences of such a calling.

Personally, as someone who is currently balancing several part-time roles, including church ministry, with raising young children, I find great challenge and also great comfort in Ashoor's words about a multivocational calling. I know I will continue to reflect on how I understand my various work roles and family life as an integrated calling. My own wrestling with how all the pieces fit together has been sifted through the words of the research candidates for the Canadian Multivocational Ministry Project that I had the privilege to listen to as I did some of the transcribing work on the project.

The candidates who shared their lives with the Canadian Multivocational Ministry Project reflected on their ministries and the other vocations in their lives, as well as the interactions between these roles. They reflected on how those roles fit together and how the job outside of pastoral ministry was positive or negative. Some reflected on how their job was just a job—for example, one interviewee who works with his hands expressed, "[My job] is one of those things which is an example of me serving in a role that I have significant skills in, but it is very much not suited to who I am . . . you know, as who God created me to be, if that makes sense. And I think that's the hard part." In other cases, the participants reflected

PART 4 | ISSUES ARISING FROM MULTIVOCATIONAL MINISTRY

on the meaning and calling of their multiple jobs as deeply intertwined commitments. For example, Catherine Gitzel described her work with Holocaust survivors with significant emotion, expressing the calling to that work alongside her church ministry position:[4]

> So, I understand my work as having meaning and purpose. Yeah, and I understand my work as being for the greater good of humanity. And I understand my work as being a calling that God has given me—the gifts and abilities and the passions that have invited me to use them in ministry and not in ministry . . . . So, there are times that I would say, Do I want to give up my part-time role? Because it's not the one that's going to grow and increase in hours anyways. And I always am like, no. And so, why not is because I don't want my life to become—I want to use the right words, so don't quote me on the wrong words—I don't want to become tunneled . . . . I want to make sure that I can take my faith . . . [that] I can take the being of who Jesus desires me to be to the other. And so, when I work with Holocaust survivors, it just somehow grounds me in saying the church has also been the perpetrator. And we have used God's name in really, really wrong ways . . . . And so, I believe I get to become an agent of change and agent of love for some of our darkest times as Christians.

Here, we see that the calling to multiple vocations that Dr. Yousif described is very evident in how Catherine Gitzel understands her work. There is no need to create a dichotomy between her work inside and outside of the church.

Hearing the story of Dr. Ashoor Yousif as he draws attention to the importance of a calling to the multivocational life, not just a calling to the spiritual work found within that multivocational life, brings forward the theme of unique fit that surfaced in the Canadian Multivocational Ministry Project. As tentmakers described their unique combination of work and ministry, it became evident that these combinations are anything but simple, expected, or straightforward. They used creativity

---

4. According to community-based research principles, interviewees were given the option to have their names associated with their quotes if they so desired (rather than anonymity).

to shape a complex life that pushes back on the unnecessary dichotomy of ministry or career.

Questions for Reflection

1. In what ways have you been challenged or encouraged to grow from within your congregation? Has that contributed to your ability to minister in the multiple areas where you invest your life?
2. Have you mentored others and empowered them by placing them in ministries that fit their gifting and whole life context? If so, what have you learned in that process?
3. How have you felt tension about your "calling" in relation to various aspects of your life?

Bibliography

Watson, James W., et al. *Canadian Multivocational Ministry Project: Research Report.* 2020. https://www.canadianmultivocationalministry.ca/report.